Mermaids
Coloring Book

Adult Colouring Books

Aryla Publishing 2017

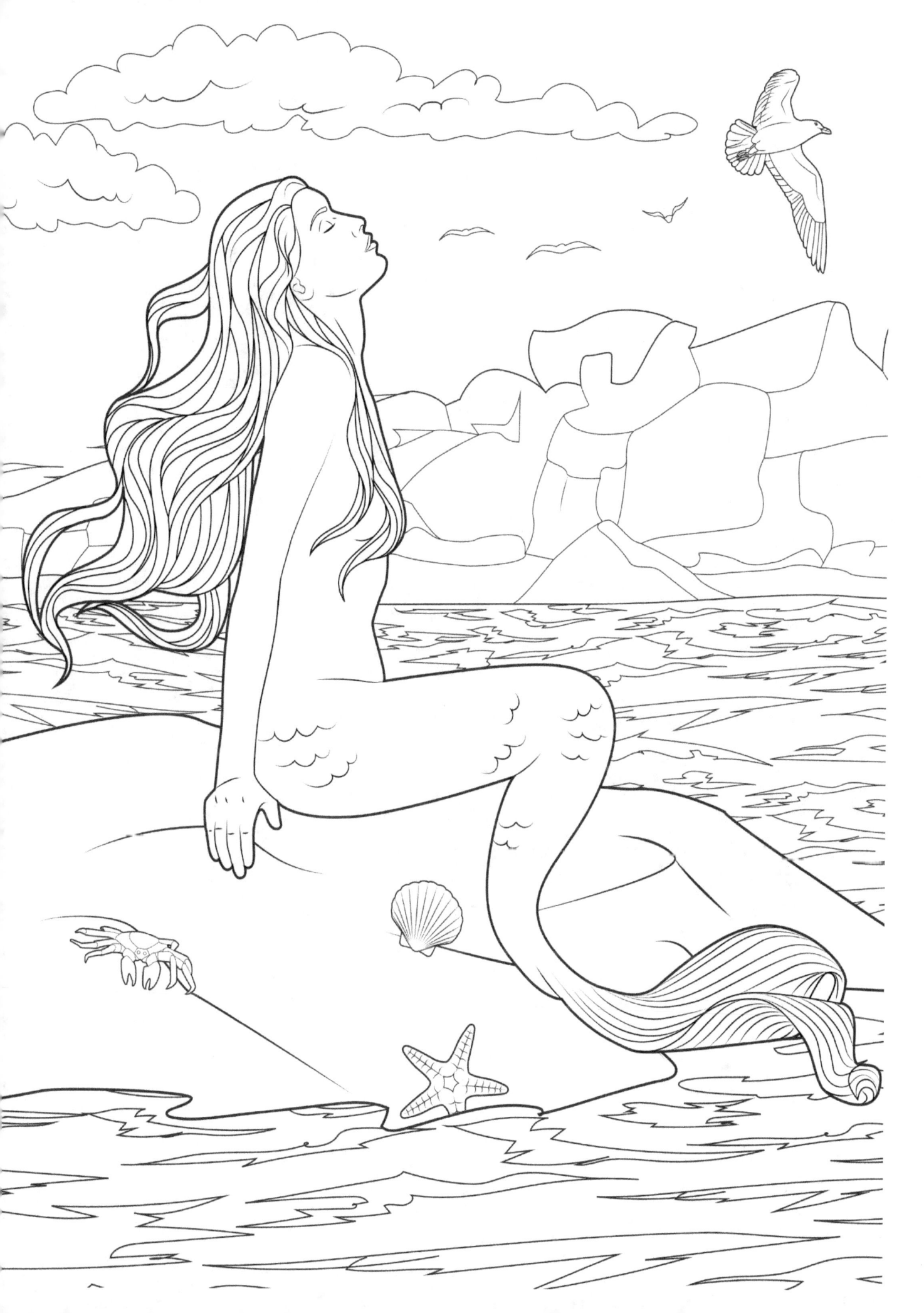

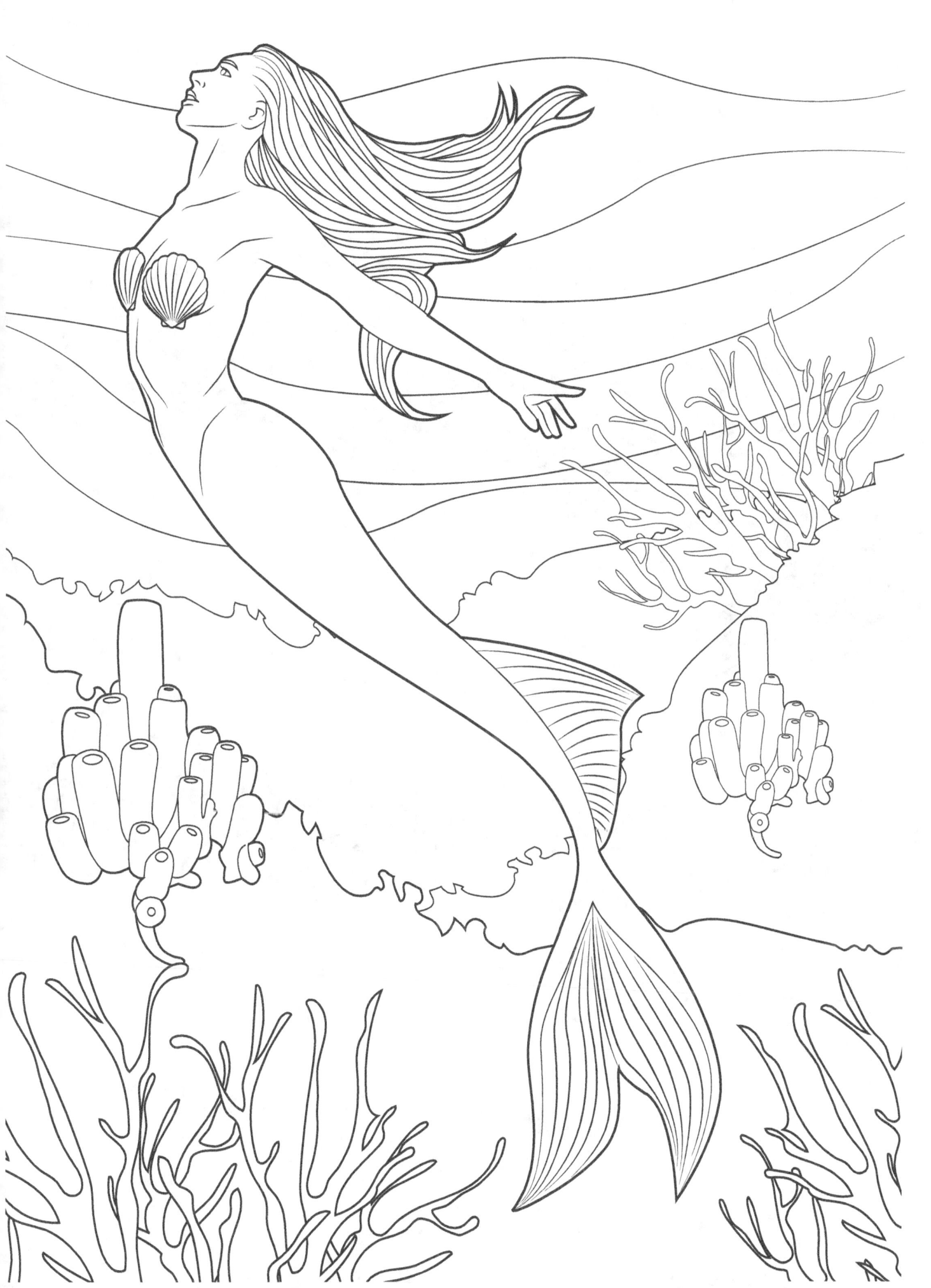

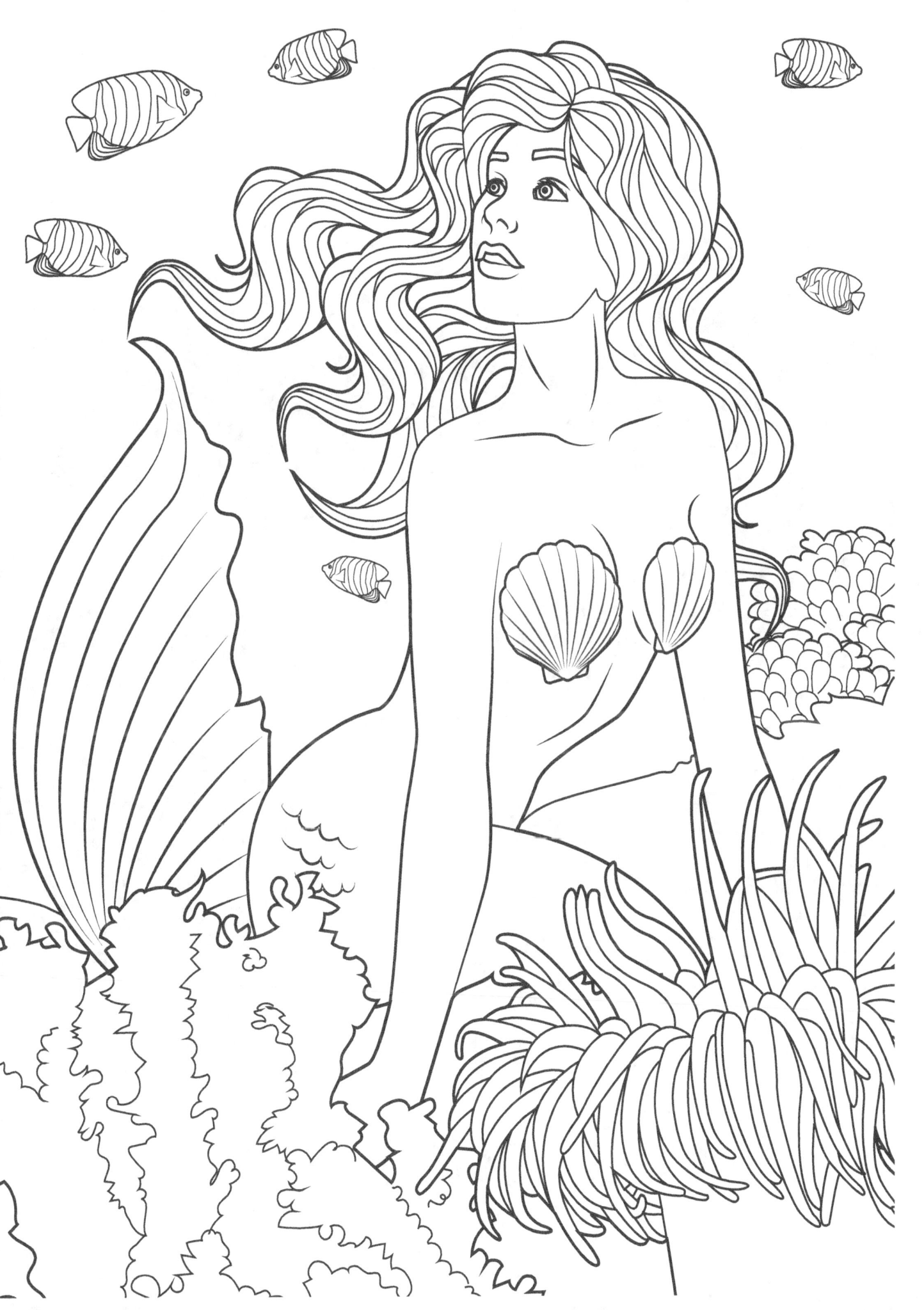

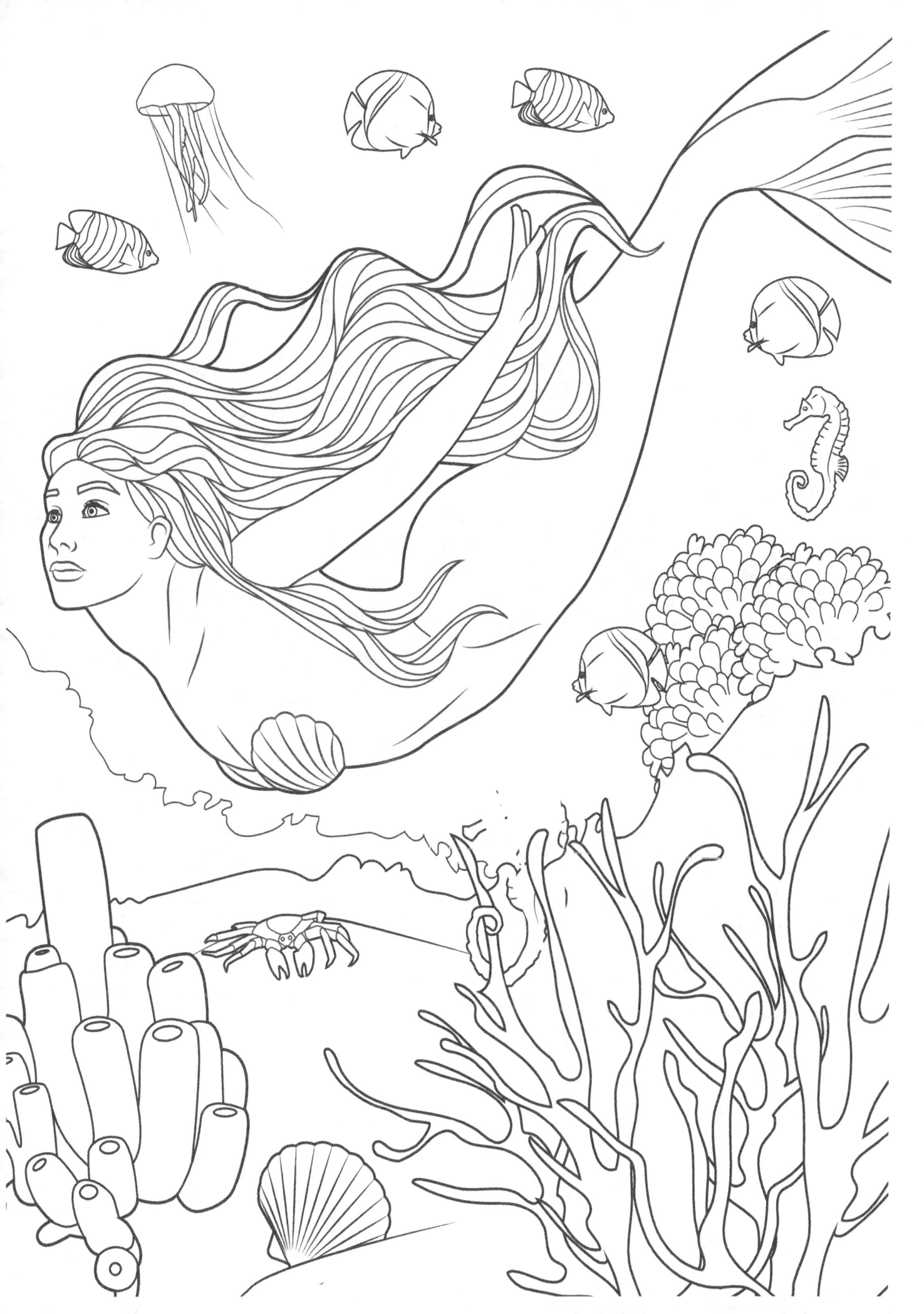

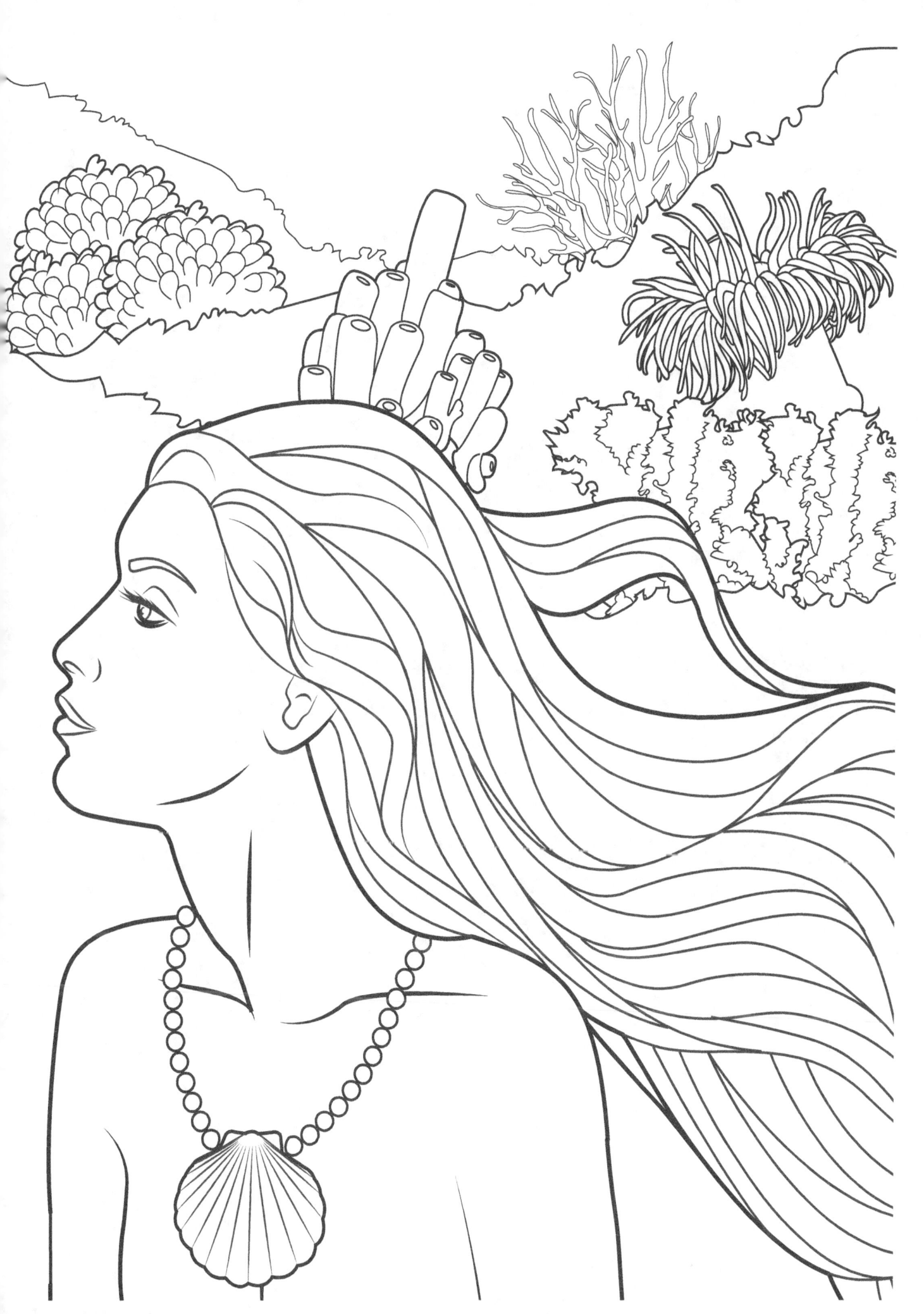

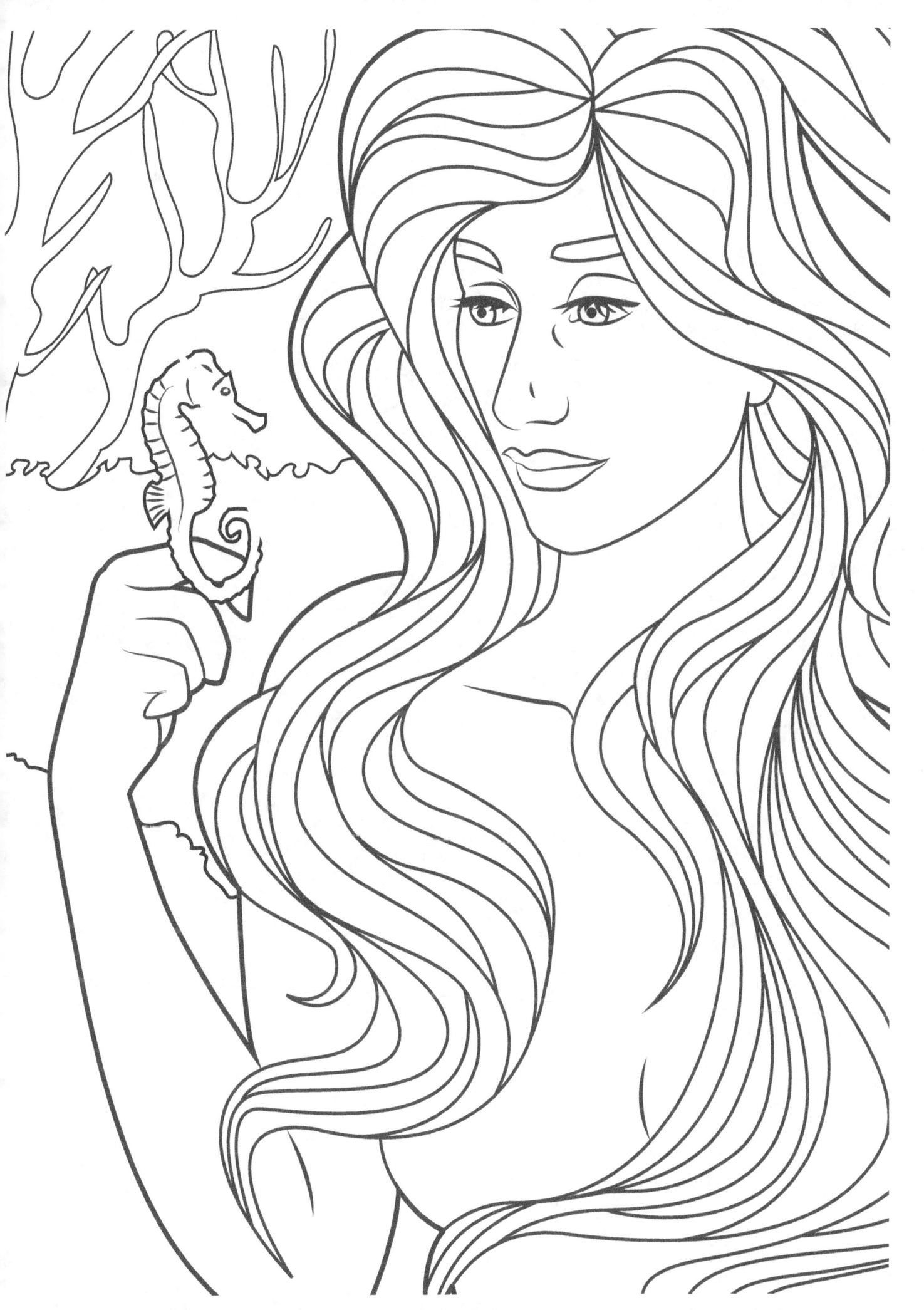

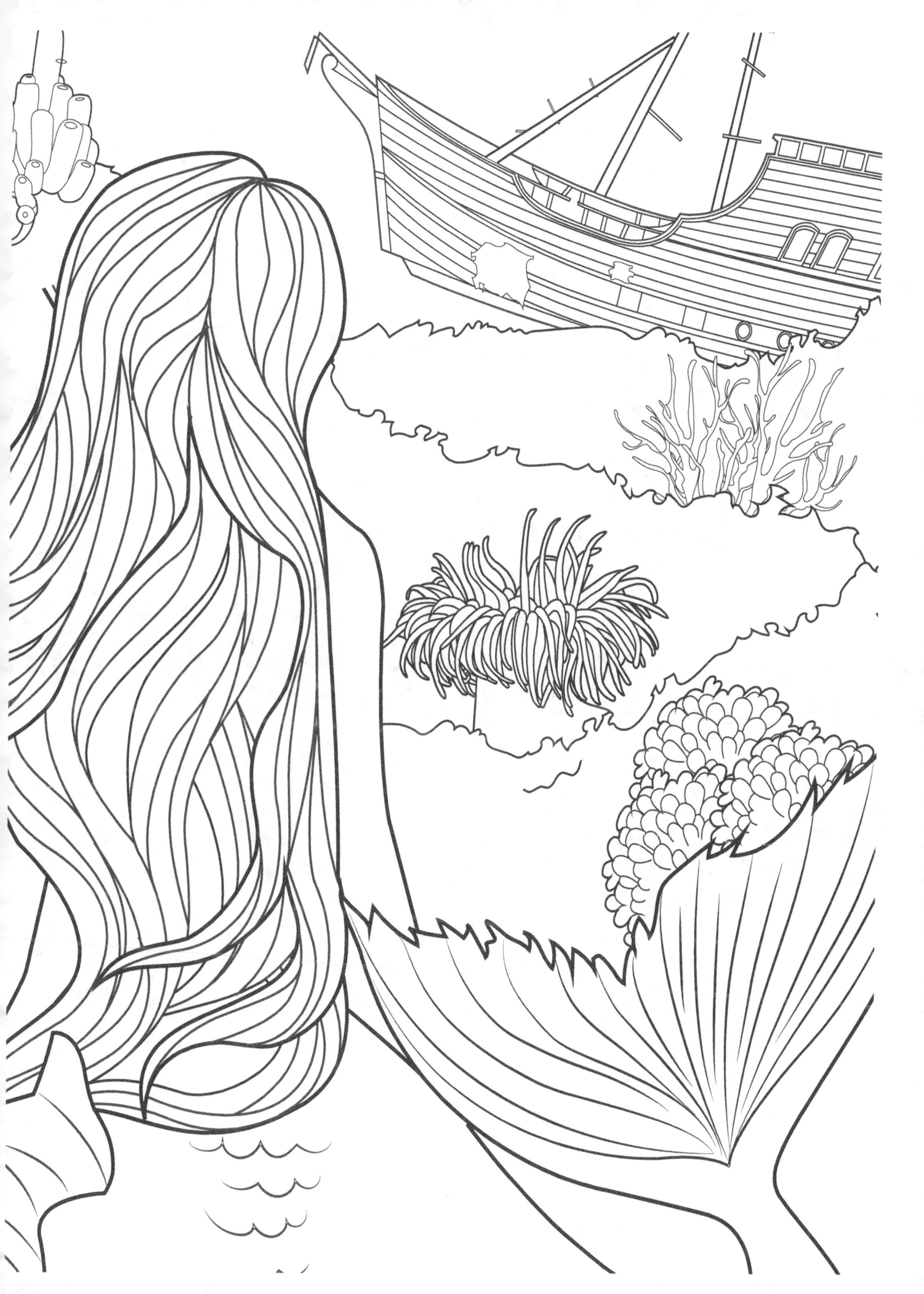

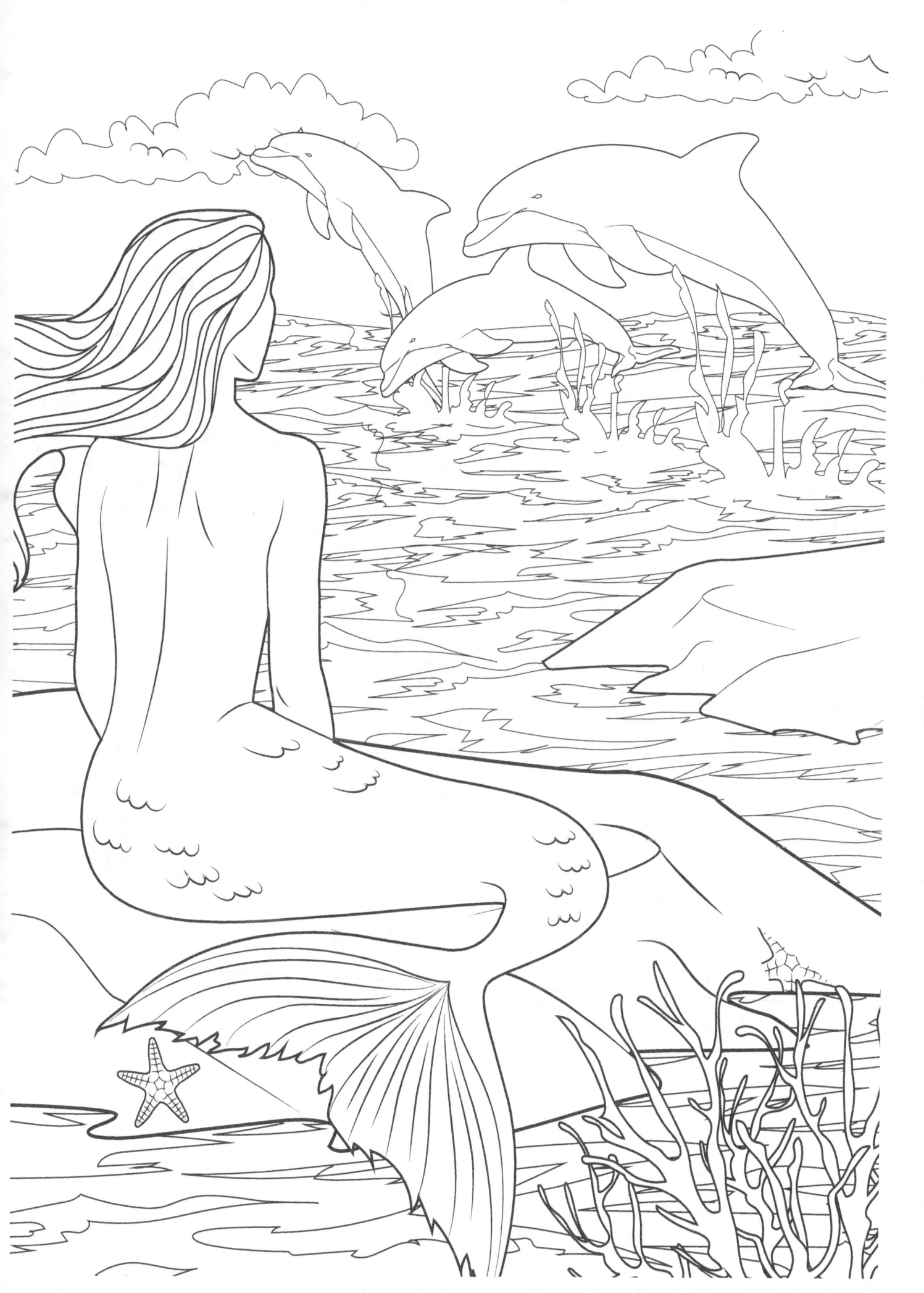

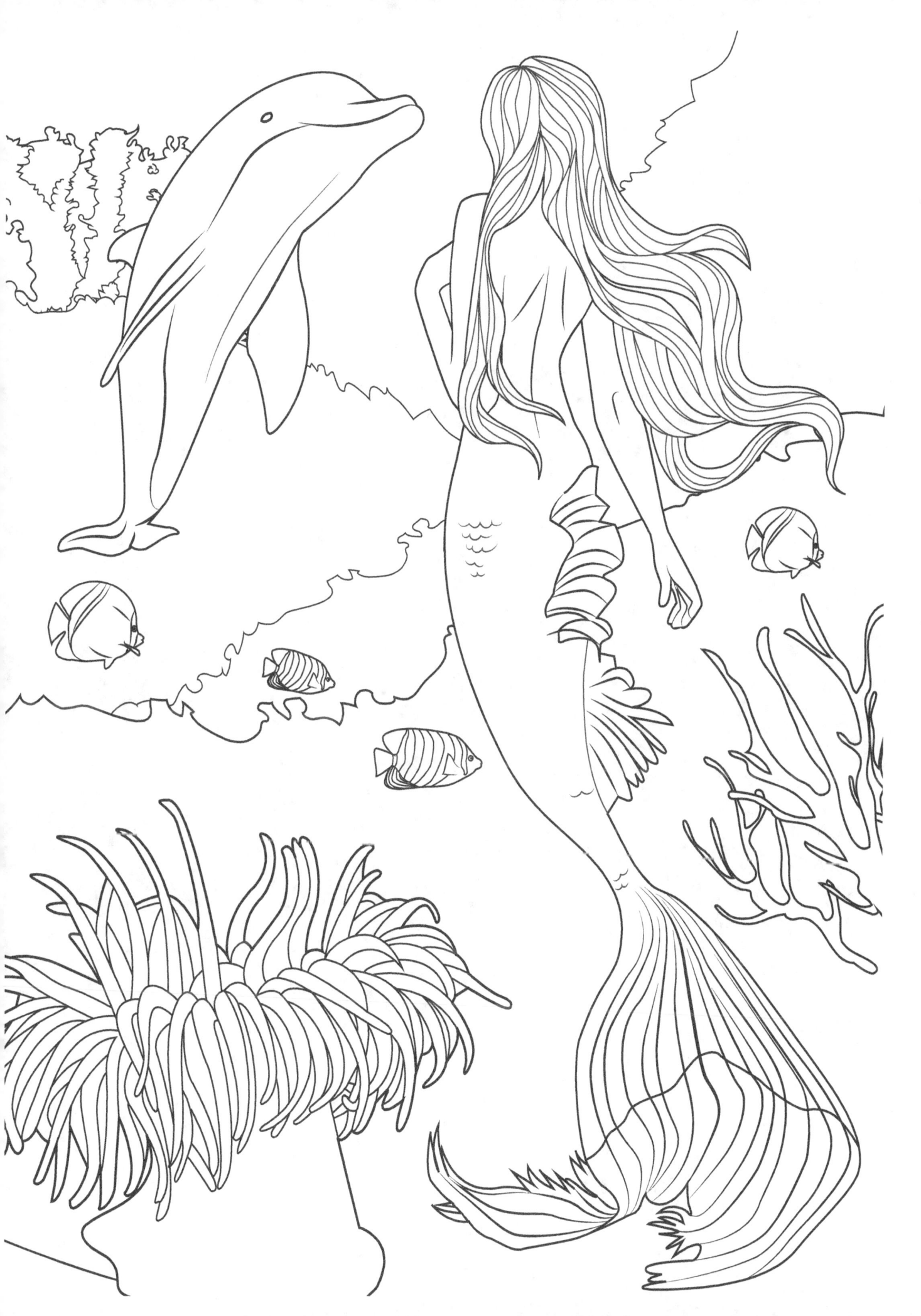

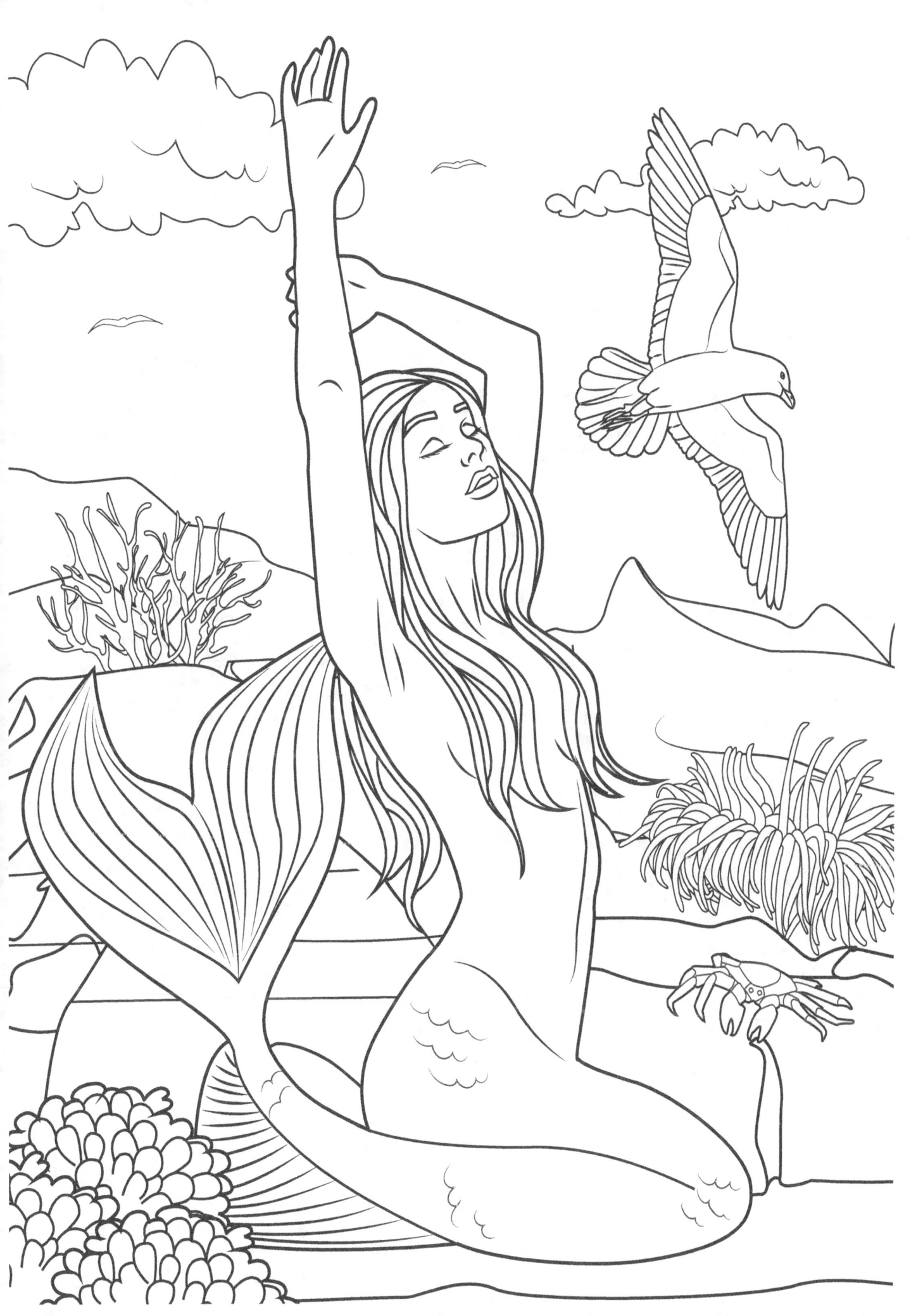

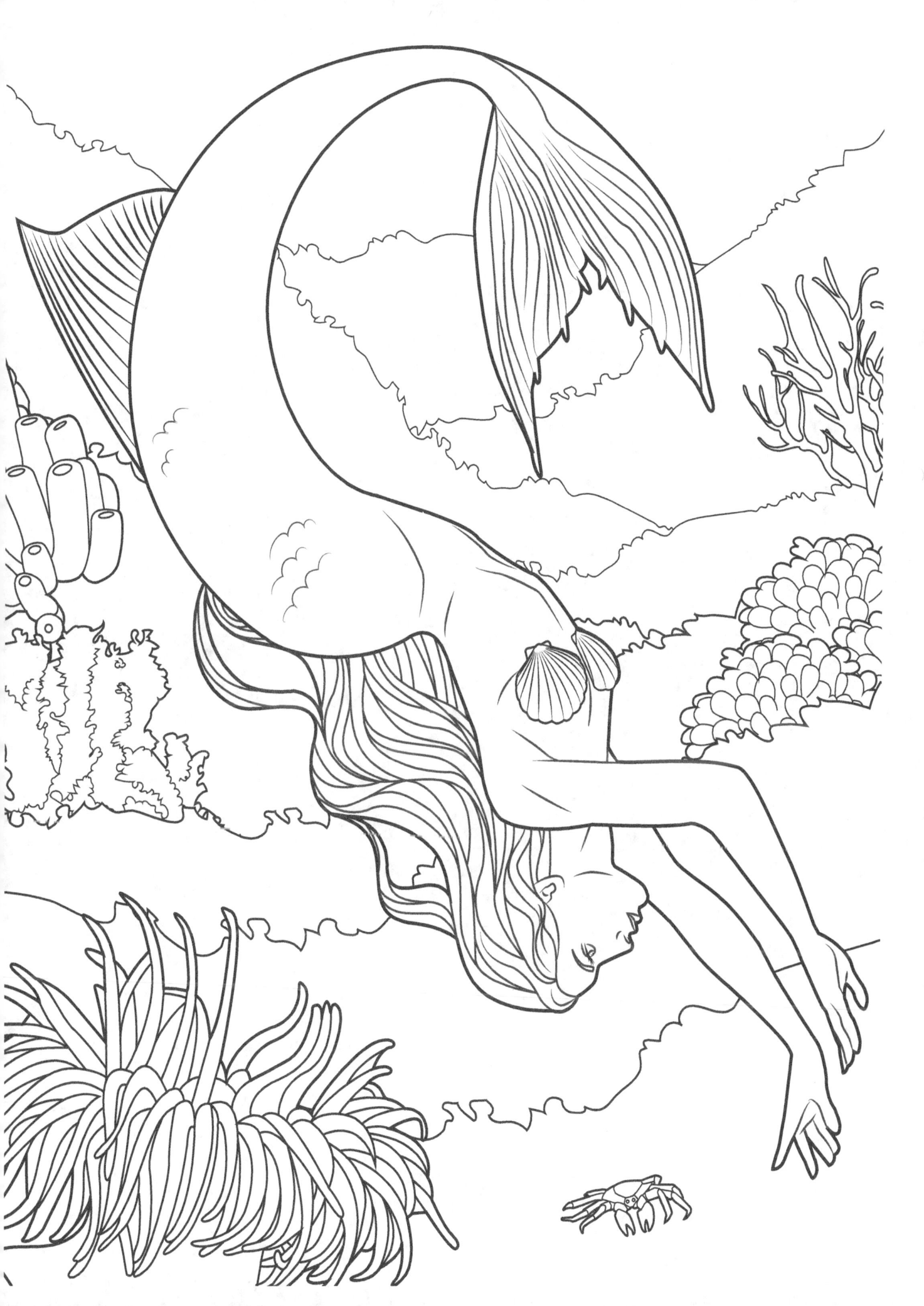

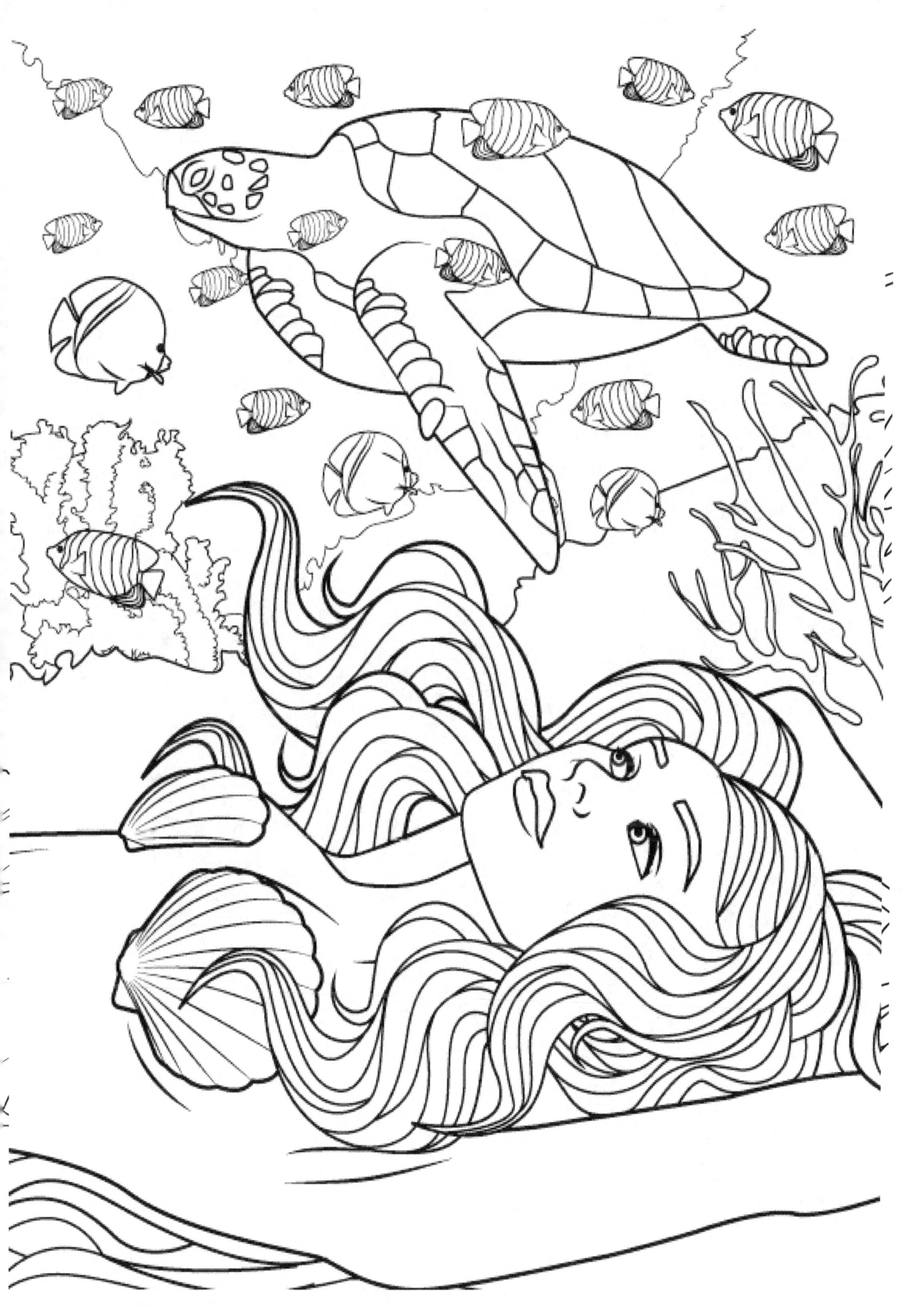

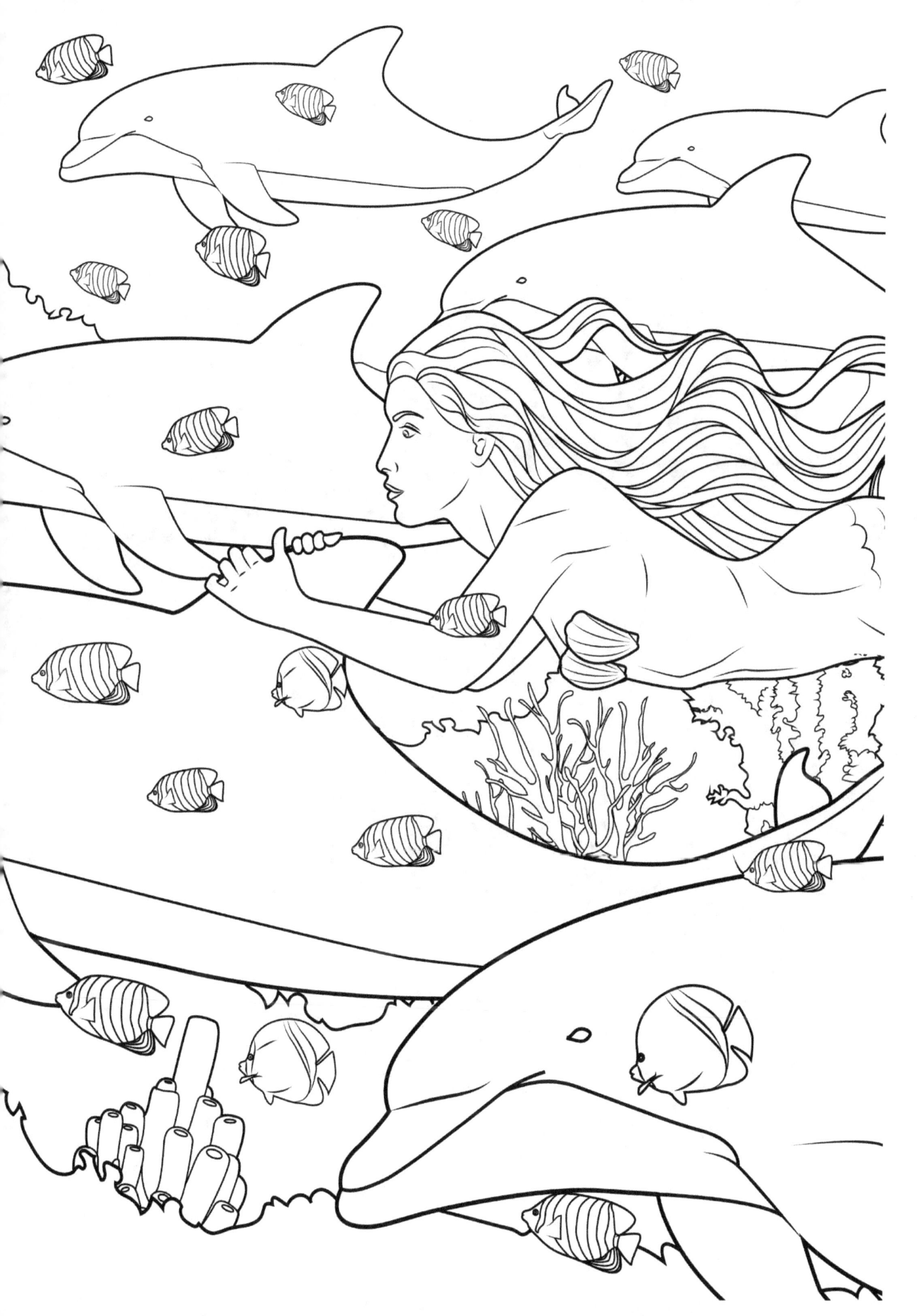

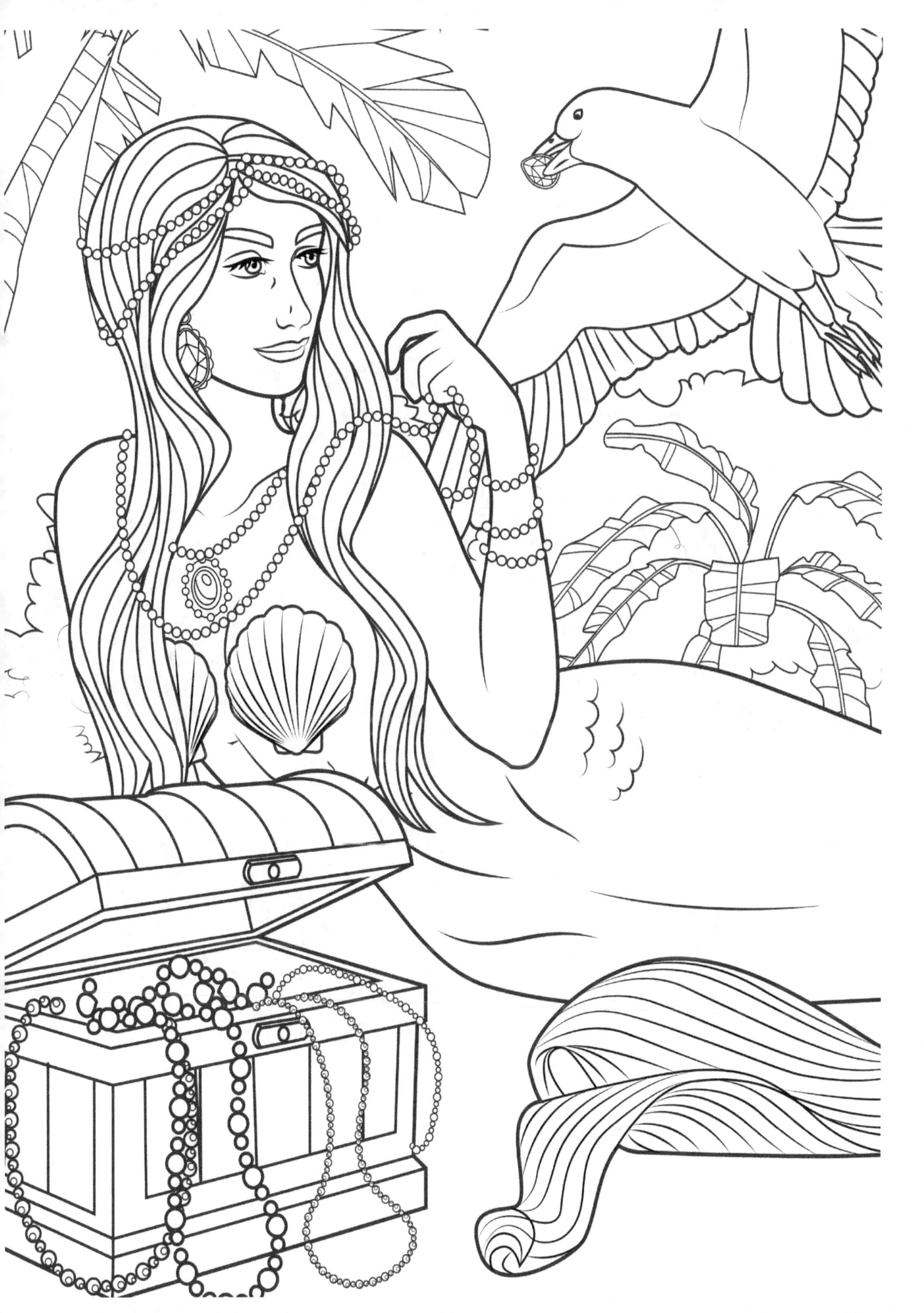

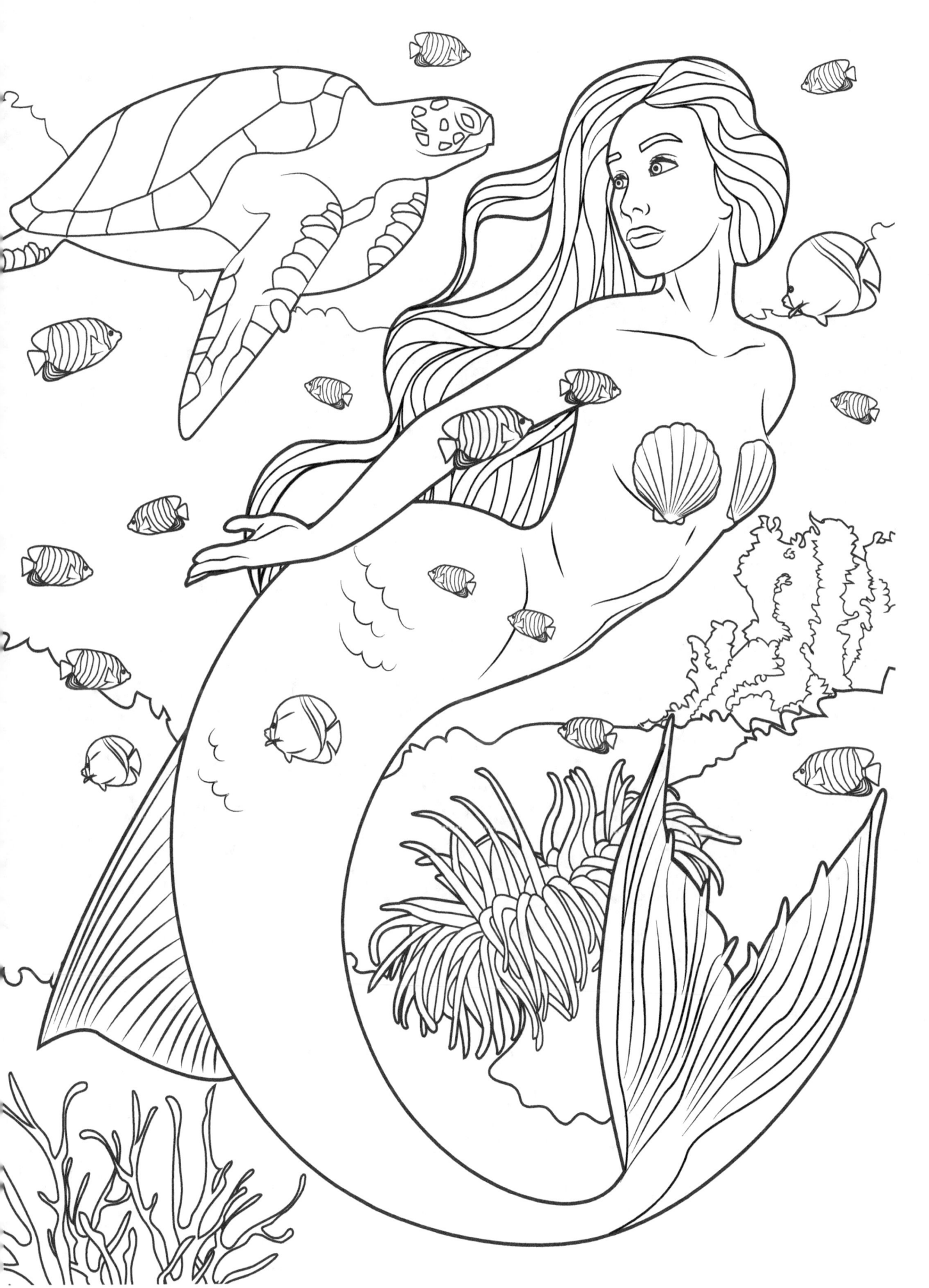

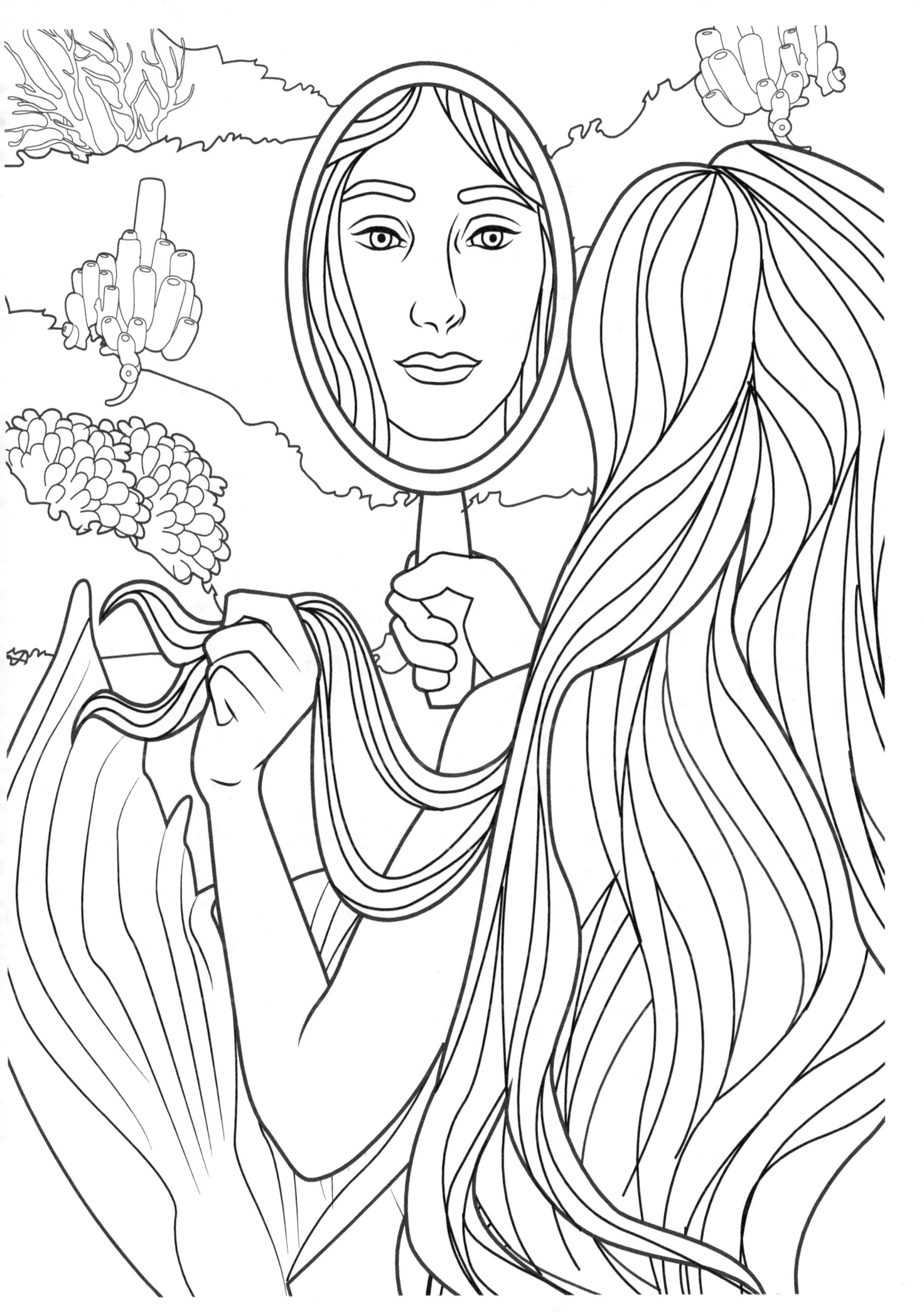

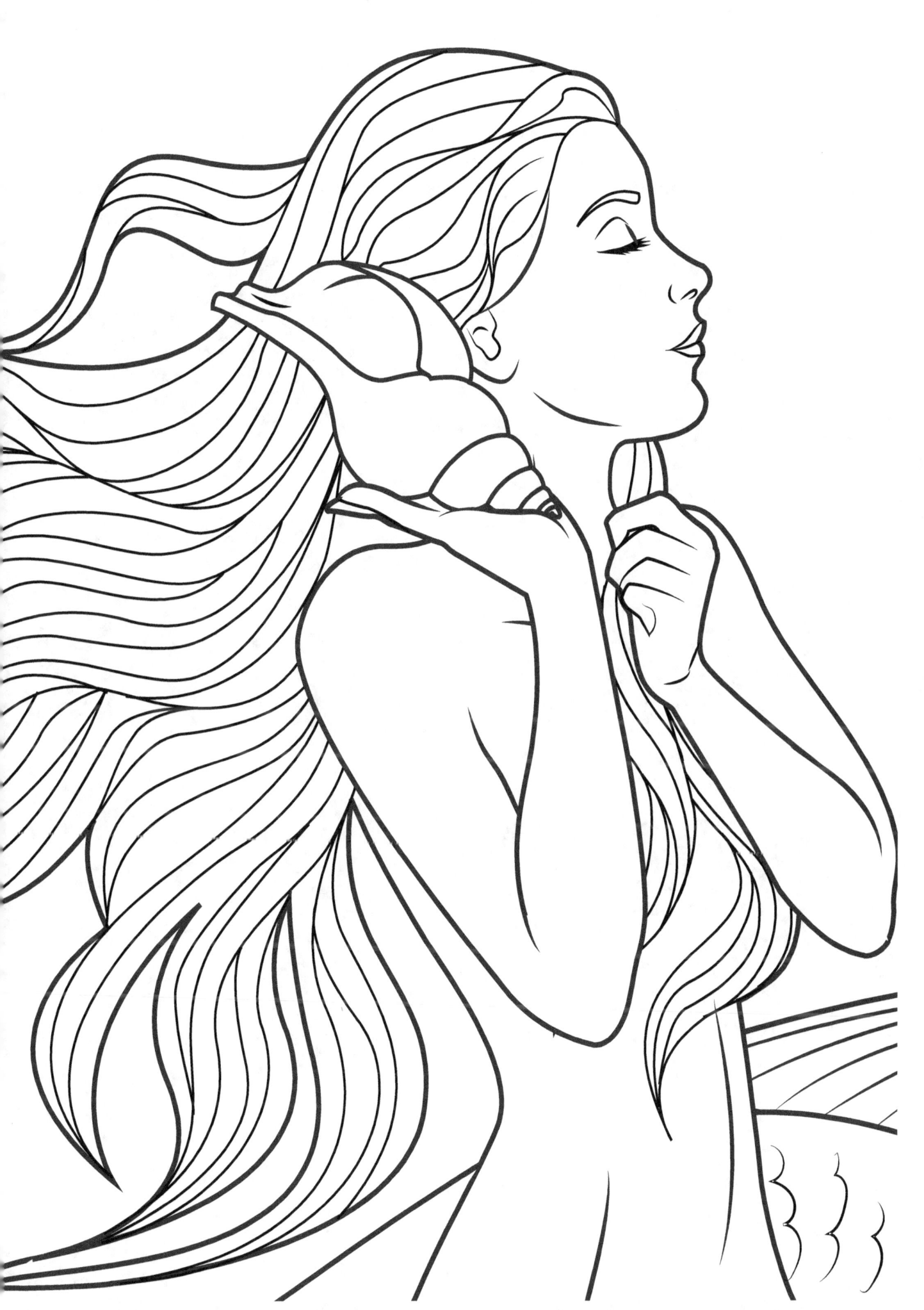

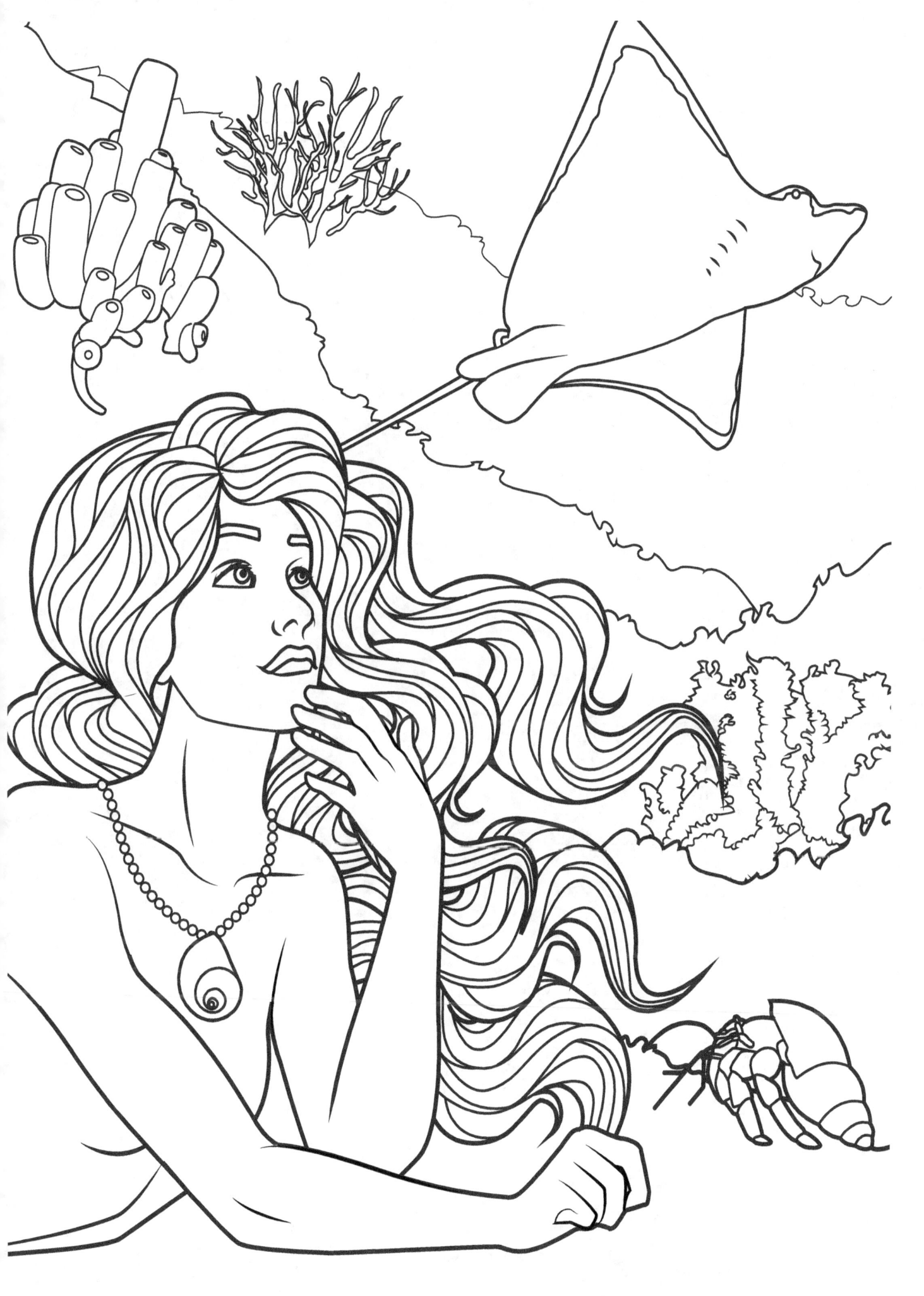

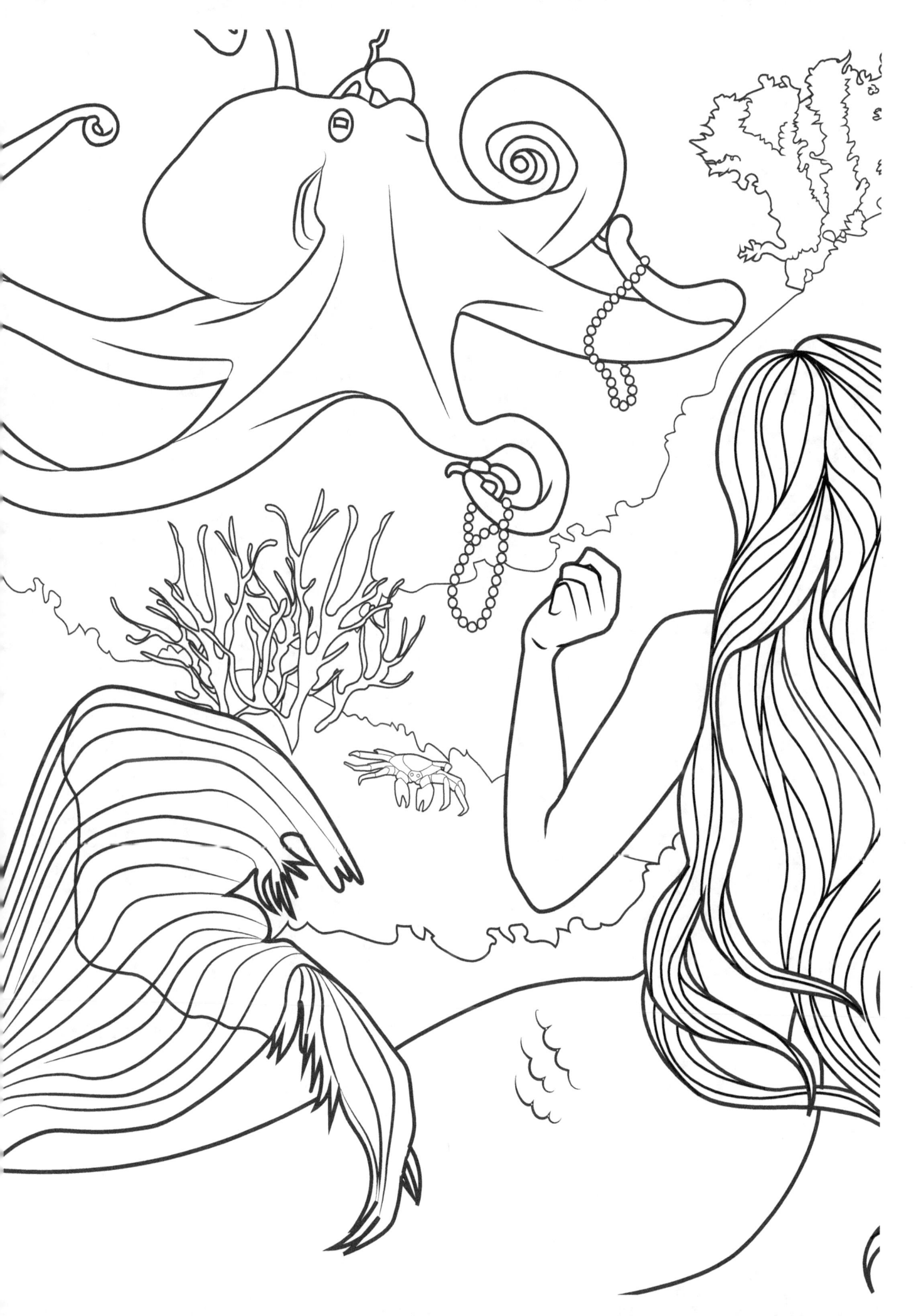

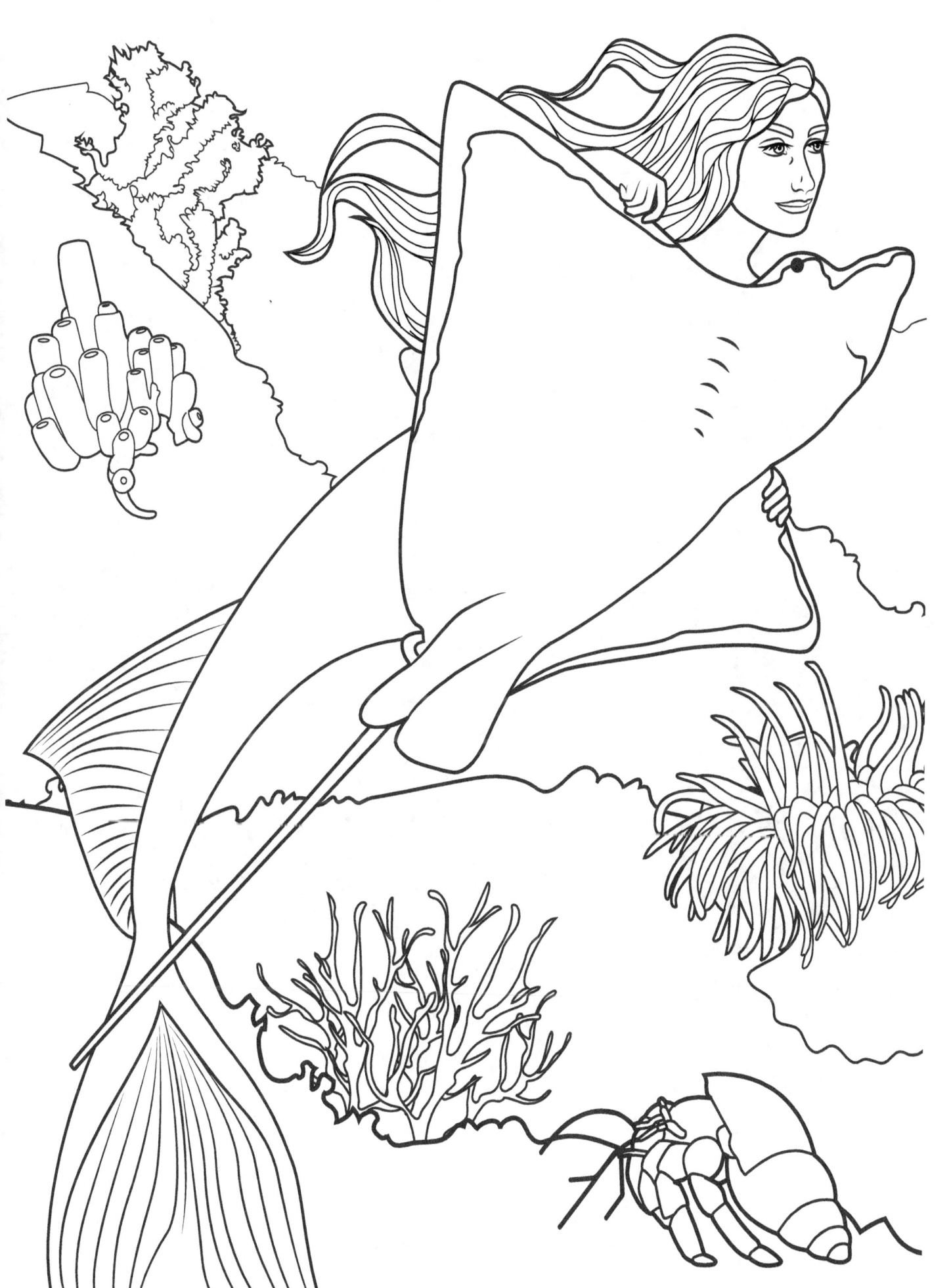

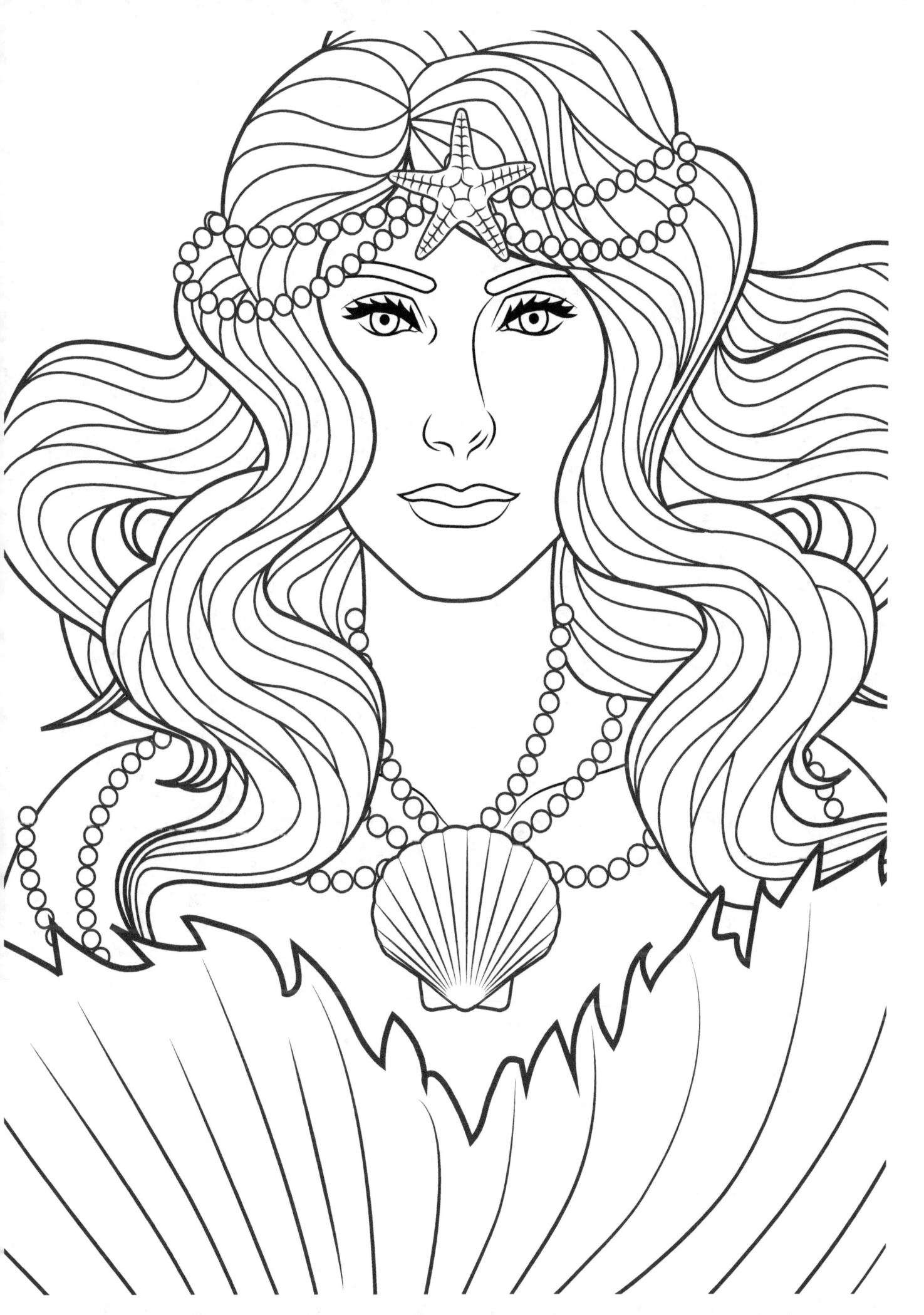

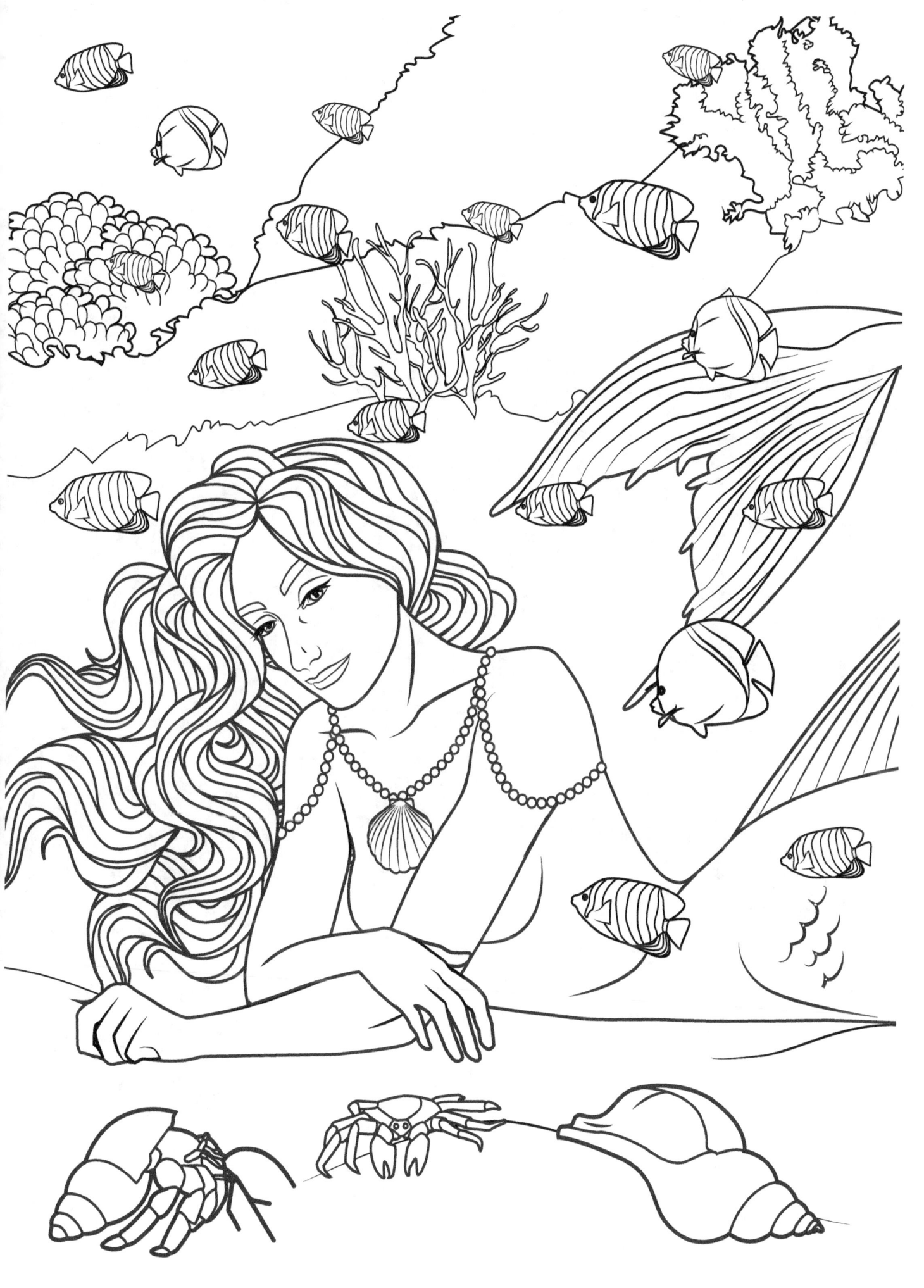

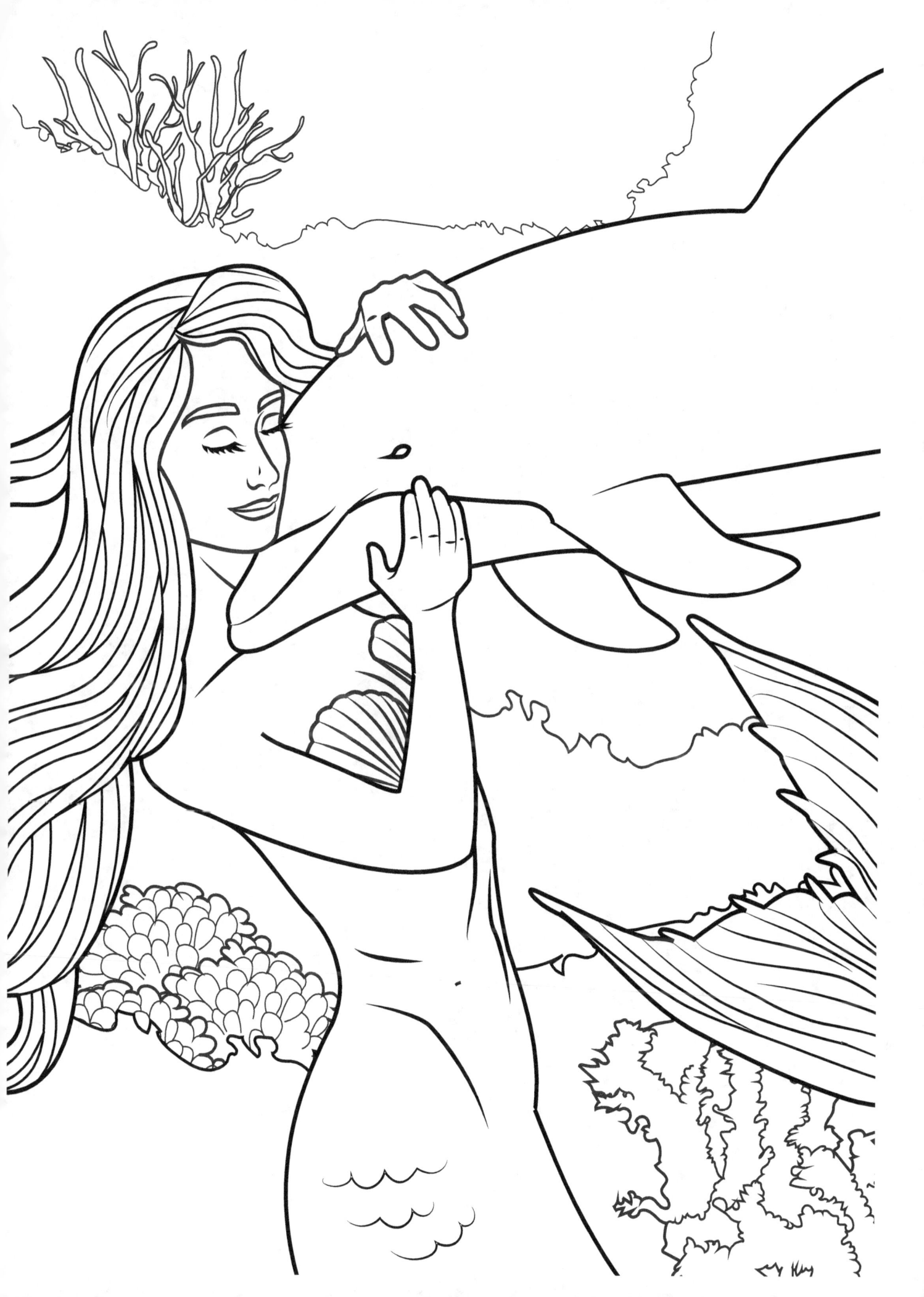

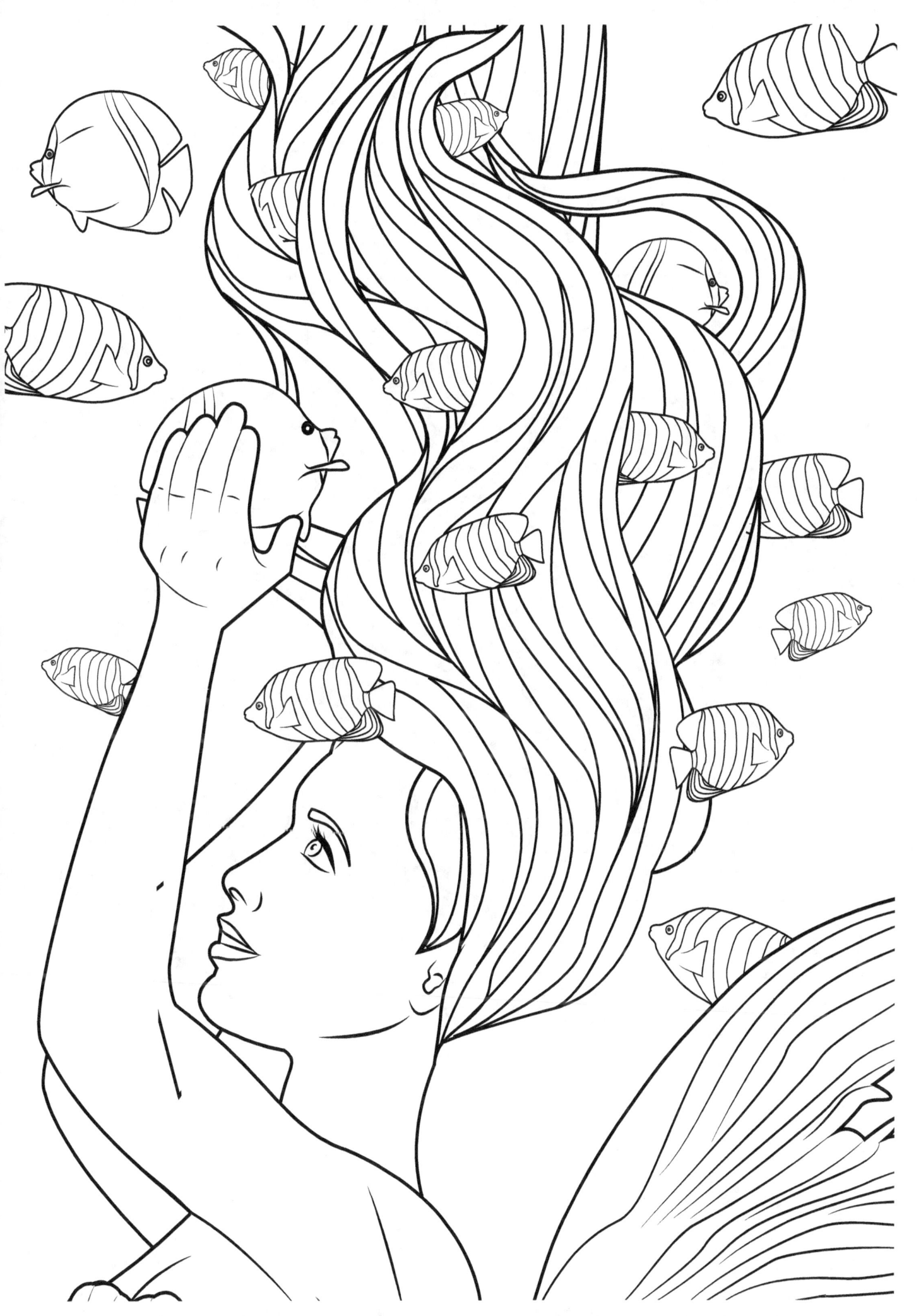

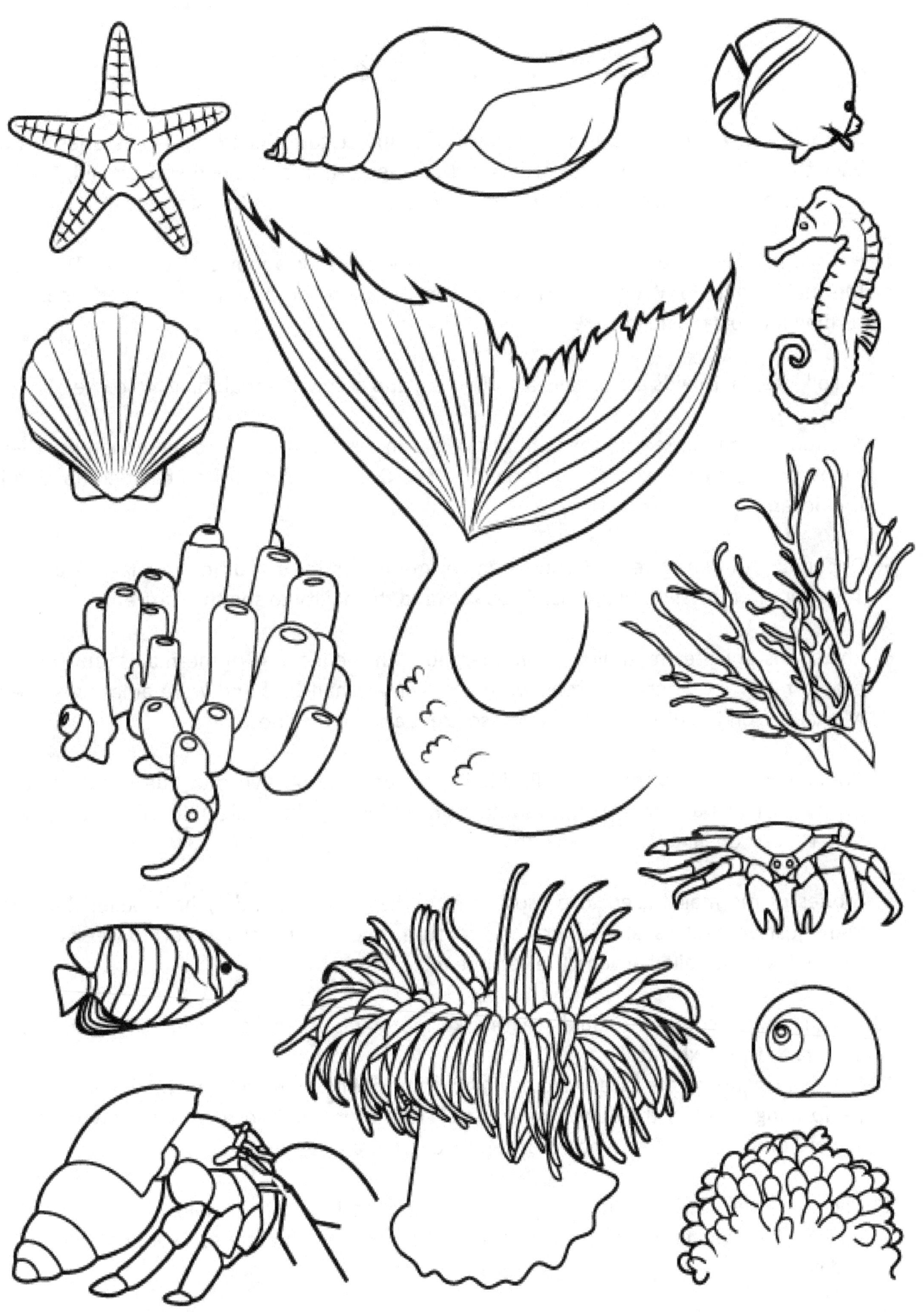

Mermaid Facts

1. Mermaids have appeared in the folklore of many cultures, with the first stories dating back to 1000 BC from Syria. According to the legend Atargatis, the first mermaid, tried to dive into a lake to become a fish, but only her bottom half was transformed.

2. Hans Christian Andersen wrote the most famous story about a mermaid, 'The Little Mermaid', in 1836. It was a dark story, and Disney made a number of changes before turning it into a movie in 1989.

3. In Folklore, mermaids are usually a bad omen, and a sign of awful things to come.

4. The most common reason for sightings of mermaids are thought to be manatees. These funny, round creatures are also known as 'Sea Cows', and can often be seen floating in the ocean.

5. Depending on which legend you listen to, mermaids have 4 different magical powers. These are Immortality, Hypnosis, Telepathy and the ability to see the future.

6. The sirens of Greek mythology have merged with the legends of mermaids, but the two are, in fact very different. Sirens were half human, half bird and were amazing singers. Mermaids, on the other hand, are not so great at holding a note.

7. Communities that live on some Pacific Islands actually believe that humans descended from mermaids and mermen. At some point in history their tails fell off and they were able to walk on land.

8. Stories of mermaids used to be so common that it was a widely held belief that they were just as real as any other sea creature. Even Columbus reported seeing three mermaids as he sailed around the Caribbean.

9. In the 1800's, con men would create fake mermaids by using Papier Mâché to attract visitors to their exhibits.

10. Mermaid sightings are rare these days, but they still happen. In 2009, onlookers saw one performing tricks in the Ocean near Kiryat Yam in Israel. The town has now offered a reward of $1 million to anyone that can take a photograph of her.

11. There is a temple in Fukuoka, Japan, that is said to have the remains of a mermaid on display. She was found on the beach in 1222, and you can still see some of the bones today.

12. The Rhinemaidens are three mermaids who feature in the Ring Cycle Opera that was written and composed by Richard Wagner between 1848 and 1874.

13. Entertainers around the world perform, dressed as mermaids, at various attractions. The most expensive mermaid tail cost £10,000, and is worn by Linden Wolbert.

14. Mermaids are believed to be responsible for creating the gemstone Aquamarine. It is formed from their tears, and brought protection to any sailors who owned one.

15. The Assyrian goddess Astarte, the Greek goddesses Triton and Aphrodite, and the African goddess Mami Wata are all depicted as mermaids.

16. There are 4 main types of mermaid in folklore. The traditional mermaids live entirely in water. In Irish folklore mermaids can shed their skin and temporarily walk on land. There are also shape-shifting mermaids who can become human whenever they want, and there's also a form of mermaid, popular in Persian tales, who can live on land or in the water.

17. Mermaids feature in many company logos. If you look closely at the Starbucks image, you can see that it is of a two tailed mermaid.

18. The preferred weapons used by merfolk to protect themselves are tridents made from coral or whale bone, sharp shells and sharks teeth.

19. A mermaid's tail is said to change colour with her mood.

20. If you are kissed by a mermaid, you will be temporarily granted with the ability to breathe underwater.

Mermaid Word Search

Can you find all of the hidden words?

```
M U L P M H J Y S H V K P X I
U Q B T Z R C T O A Z R N F H
F J V Z N U S M N A E V N Y E
K K W J S E Q O B E V Q S X L
H X L A L K D Q C S M J R I P
A Q U A M A R I N E S B M R F
H S C W T F A P R H A M I L U
Y S T E L R N M E T O N O D I
P Z A J Y F A L L R C U S Y W
T I O E C I L Q T E N L U O H
C O W W D S O A E D R B B J Q
F T H G T H L R E N R E E J C
D E N T L E I R A U L P L Y L
Z F N P D C M G X P H I F M B
P U W G Z A R D F Y S Z L J K
```

Aquamarine	Immortal	Scales
Ariel	Mermaid	Shells
Fish	Ocean	Trident
Flounder	Prince Eric	Under The Sea

Mermaid Quiz

Questions

1. What is the name of Ariel's father in "The Little Mermaid"?
2. How many prongs does a trident spear have?
3. What is another name for a Manatee?
4. Who was tied to the mast of his ship so he could hear the Sirens' song as the boat sailed past their island?
5. In which movie did Captain Jack Sparrow meet a group of mermaids?
6. What was the name of the Assyrian goddess who was a mermaid?
7. The Blue Men of the Minch are a group of mermen who tormented ships around the coast of which country?
8. Rather than living in castles, what underwater structures do merfolk live in?
9. How do mermaids breathe underwater?
10. Where do mermaids gather most of their human artefacts?
11. In "The Little Mermaid", what does Ursula steal from Ariel and keep in a shell?
12. When they have a picnic on the rocks, what do mermaids use instead of a blanket?
13. Which colour can merfolk not see?
14. The statue of The Little Mermaid in Copenhagen harbour is made from which material?
15. Jodi Benson was the voice of Ariel in the Disney animation of The Little Mermaid, but which character did she provide the voice for in Toy Story 2?
16. How do mermaids communicate without speaking out loud?
17. Mermaids have the top half of a human and the bottom half of what creature?
18. The Combs and Mirrors that mermaids are often seen with are linked to which Roman Goddess of love?
19. Lara, the Amazonian water spirit, is a mermaid who lives around which continent?
20. Where was Columbus when he reportedly saw a group of mermaids?

Mermaid Crossword

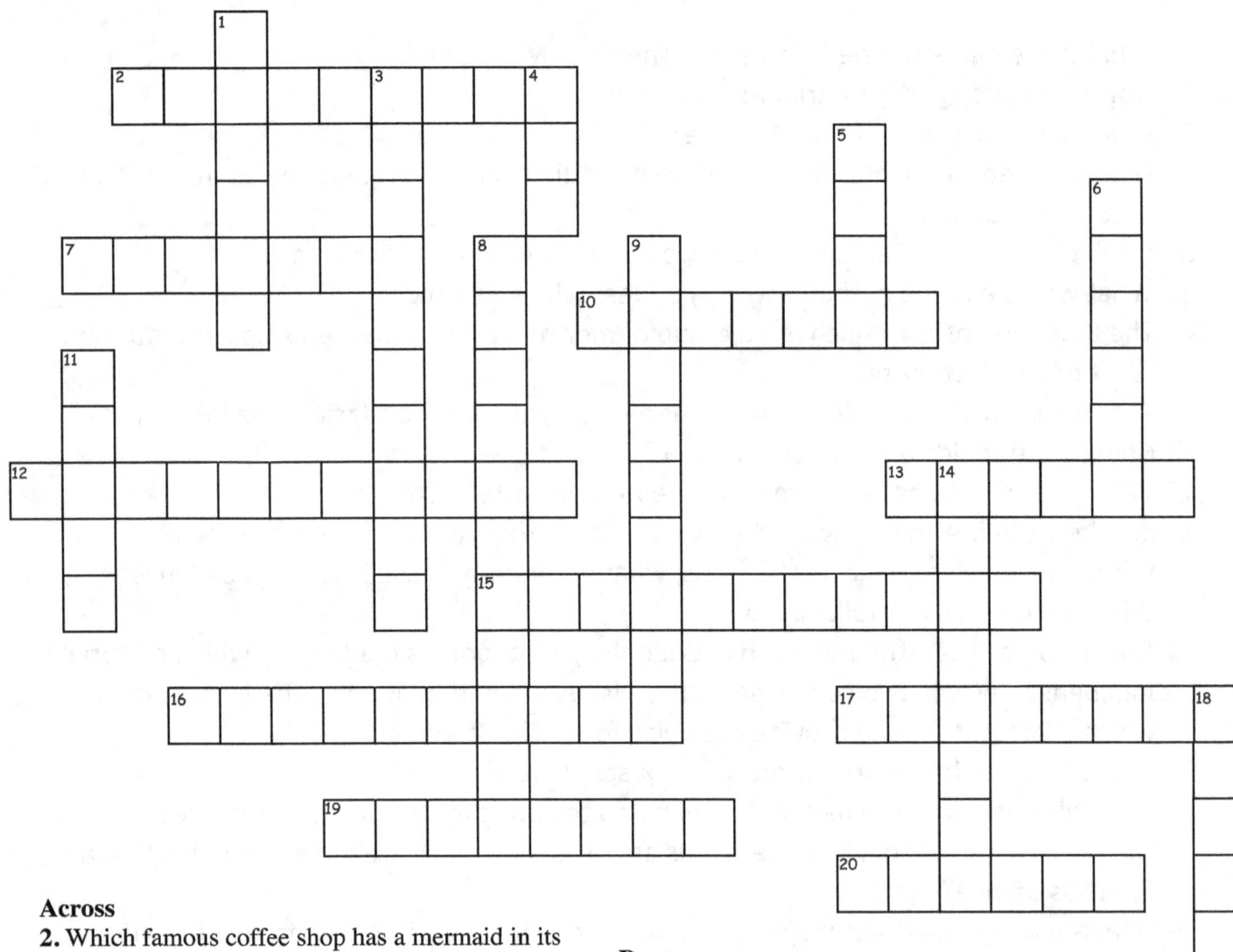

Across

2. Which famous coffee shop has a mermaid in its logo? (9)

7. The creature that is thought to have been mistaken for a mermaid by early seafarers (7)

10. The collective name for all of the mermaids and mermen (7)

12. Which boy wizard encountered mermaids in the second task of the Triwizard tournament? (5, 6)

13. The composer of the "Ring Cycle" music drama that featured three Rhine Daughters who were mermaids (6)

15. The paper and glue mix that was used to make mermaid hoaxes (6, 5)

16. The City where you will find a bronze statue of the Little Mermaid in the harbour (10)

17. The famous Italian explorer who, while sailing around Hispaniola, spotted 3 mermaids in 1493 (8)

19. Hans Christian _____ , the author of the Little Mermaid Fairy tale in 1836 (8)

20. The name of the sea witch from the Little Mermaid Movie (6)

Down

1. The Polish City with a mermaid on its Coat of Arms (6)

3. A kiss from a mermaid will allow you to breathe where? (10)

4. The meaning of the word "Mer" (3)

5. Which part of a mermaid changes colour with their mood? (4)

6. Mermaids can apparently predict the what? (6)

8. The playwright who mentioned mermaids in two of his plays The Comedy of Errors and The Tempest (11)

9. The name of the singing crab from The Little Mermaid Movie (9)

11. Aquamarine is a gemstone that many believe is created by a mermaid's _____ (5)

14. This Greek Hero, with a weakness in his heel, was born to a mermaid (8)

18. The name of the Greek sea-nymphs who lured sailors to their island by singing (6)

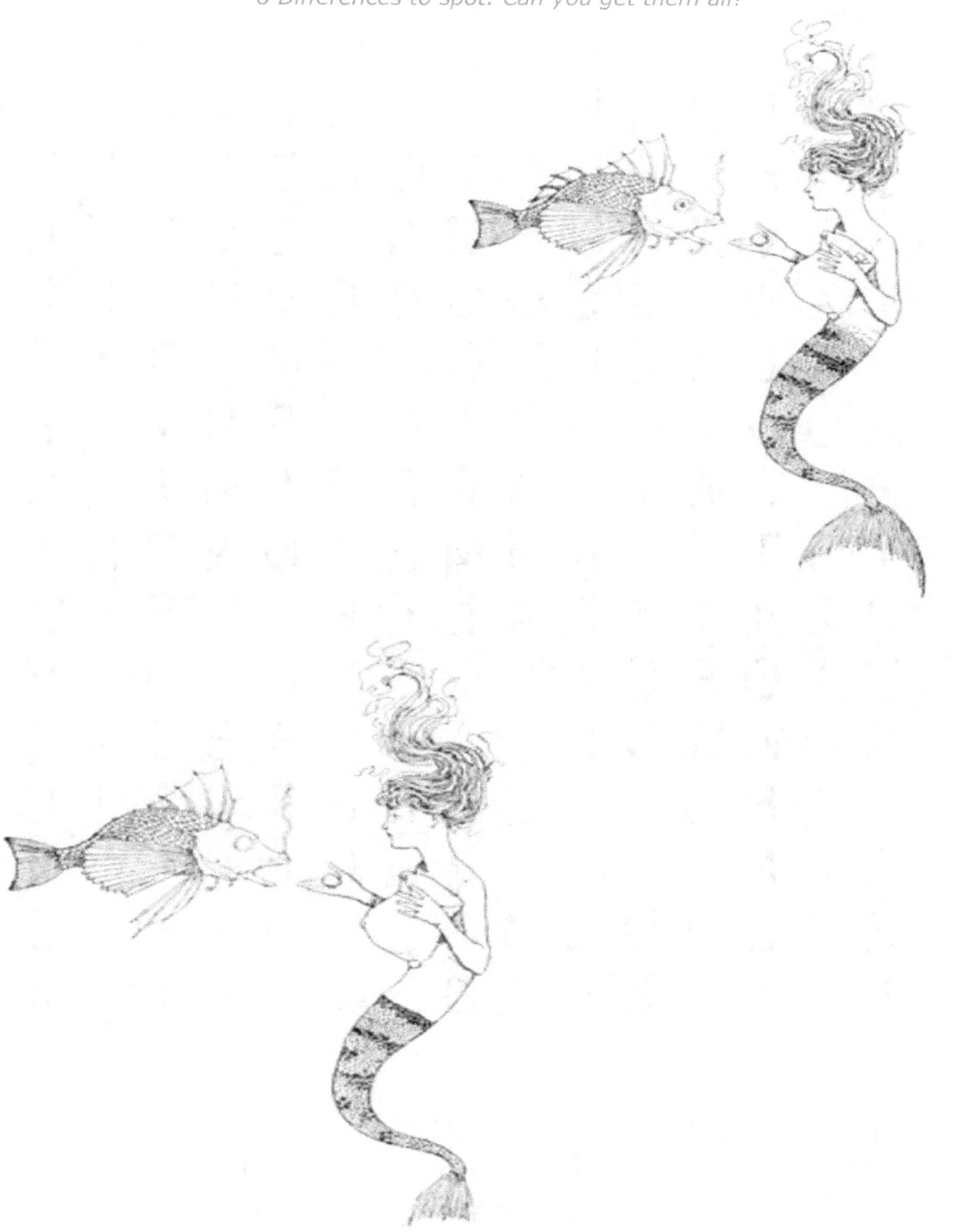

Mermaid Word Search

Can you find all of the hidden words?

```
M U L P M H J Y S H V K P X I
U Q B T Z R C T O A Z R N F H
F J V Z N U S M N A E V N Y E
K K W J S E Q O B E V Q S X L
H X L A L K D Q C S M J R I P
A Q U A M A R I N E S B M R F
H S C W T F A P R H A M I L U
Y S T E L R N M E T O N O D I
P Z A J Y F A L L R C U S Y W
T I O E C I L Q T E N L U O H
C O W W D S O A E D R B B J Q
F T H G T H L R E N R E E J C
D E N T L E I R A U L P L Y L
Z F N P D C M G X P H I F M B
P U W G Z A R D F Y S Z L J K
```

Aquamarine	Immortal	Scales
Ariel	Mermaid	Shells
Fish	Ocean	Trident
Flounder	Prince Eric	Under The Sea

Answers

1. King Triton
2. 3
3. A Sea Cow
4. Odysseus
5. Pirates of the Caribbean: On Stranger Tides
6. Atargatis
7. Scotland
8. Caves or Trenches
9. They have gills
10. Shipwrecks
11. Her Voice
12. A seaweed carpet
13. Red- It doesn't exist in the depths of the ocean
14. Bronze
15. Barbie
16. Telepathy
17. Fish
18. Venus
19. South America
20. Hispaniola in the Caribbean

Spot The Difference

1. Fish Eye
2. Fish Mouth
3. Fish Fin
4. Mermaid Scales
5. Mermaid Tail
6. Bag Contents

Thank you for purchasing this book.

If you would like to know more about Aryla Publishing Books please visit:-

www.ArylaPublishing.com

Or follow us on
Facebook
Twitter
Instagram
for *free promotions*

@arylapublishing

We would love to know what you think of this book so please leave us a review.

Have a wonderful day ☺

Other Coloring Books from Aryla Publishing

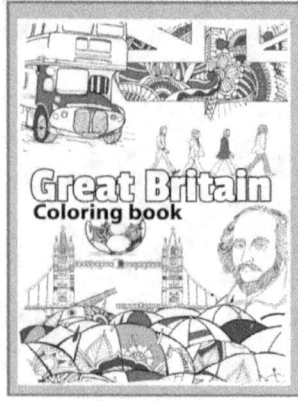 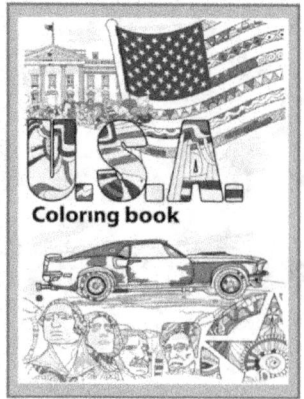 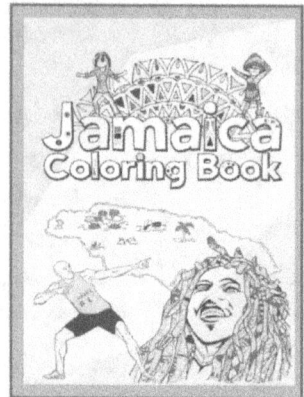 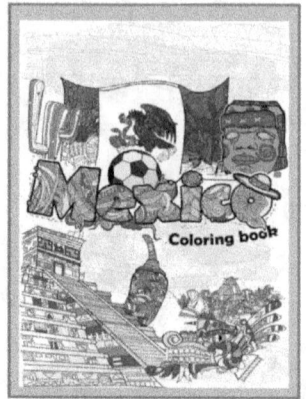

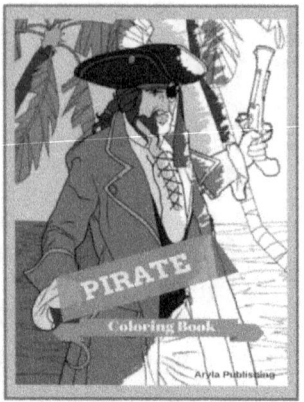 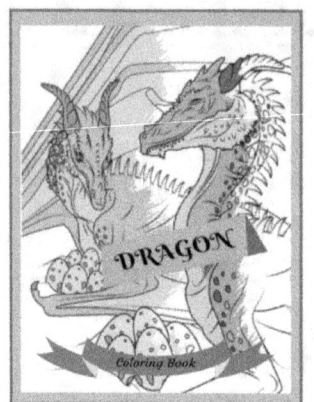 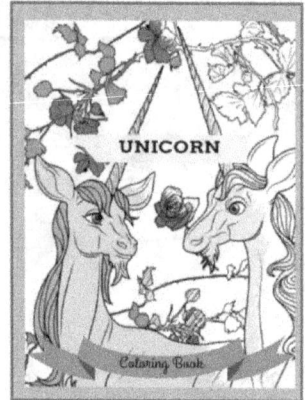 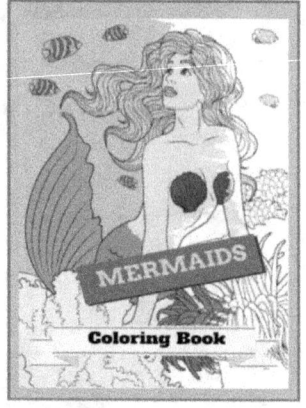

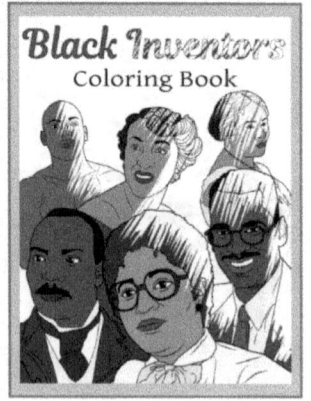 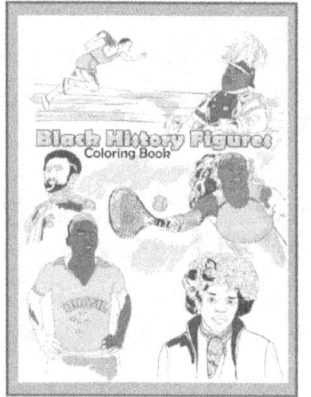 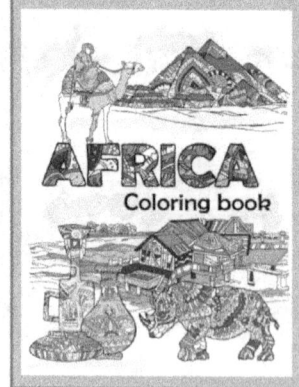 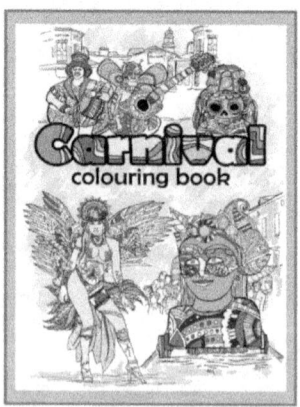

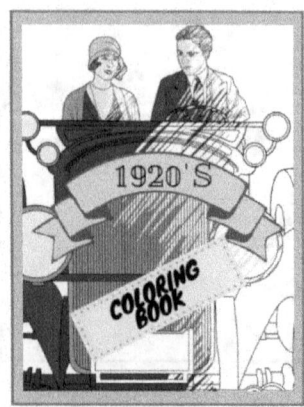 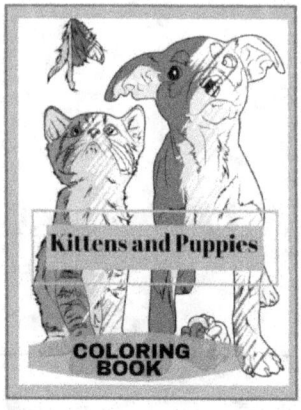 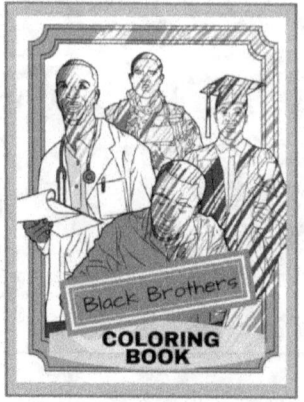 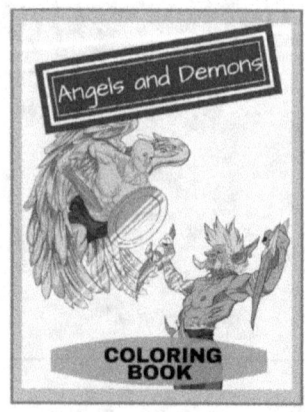

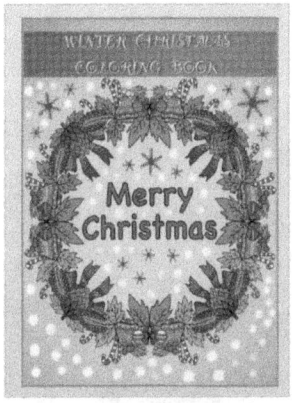

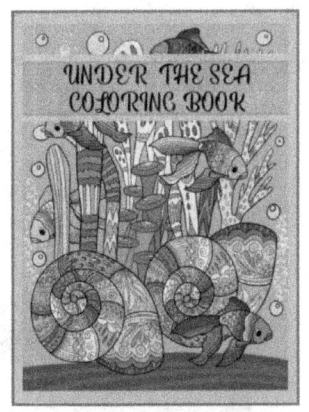

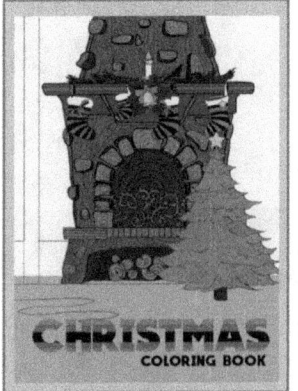

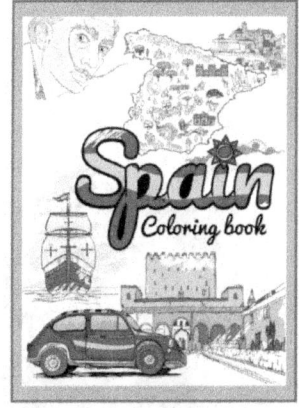

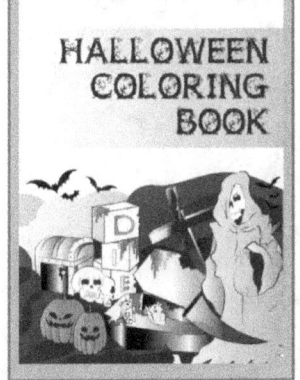

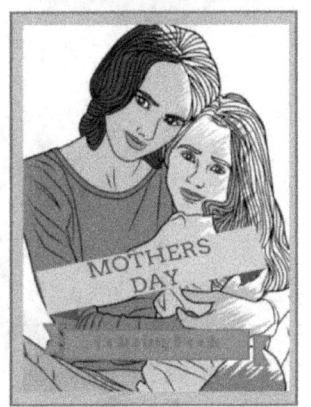

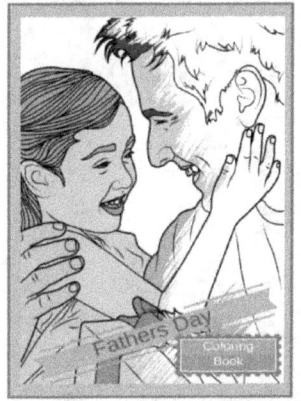

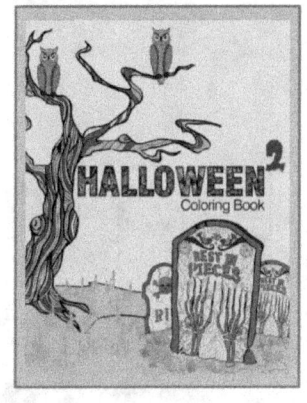

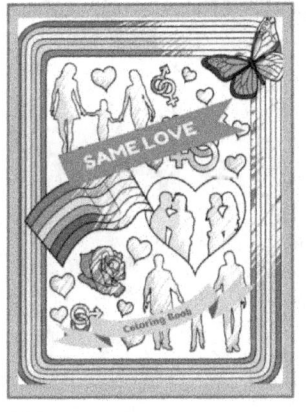

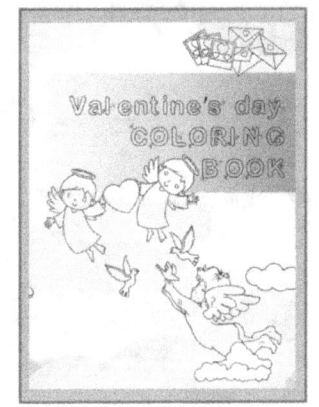

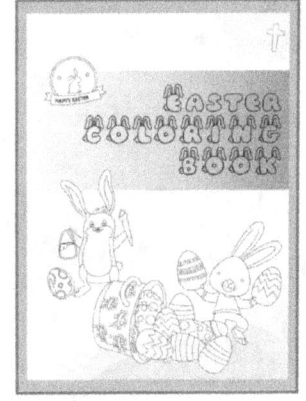

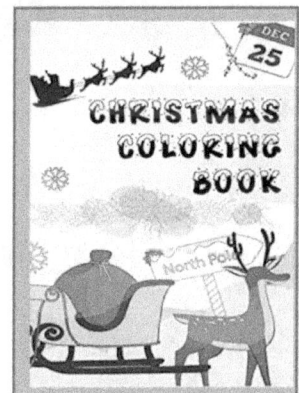

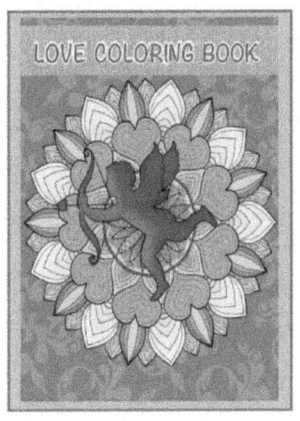

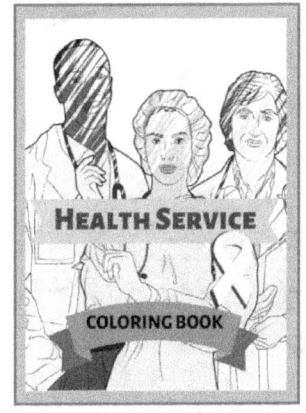

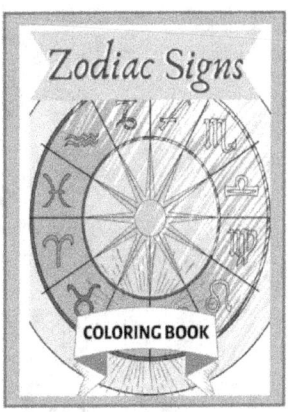

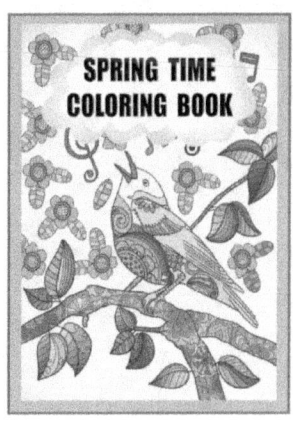

Color In Fun
Kids Books

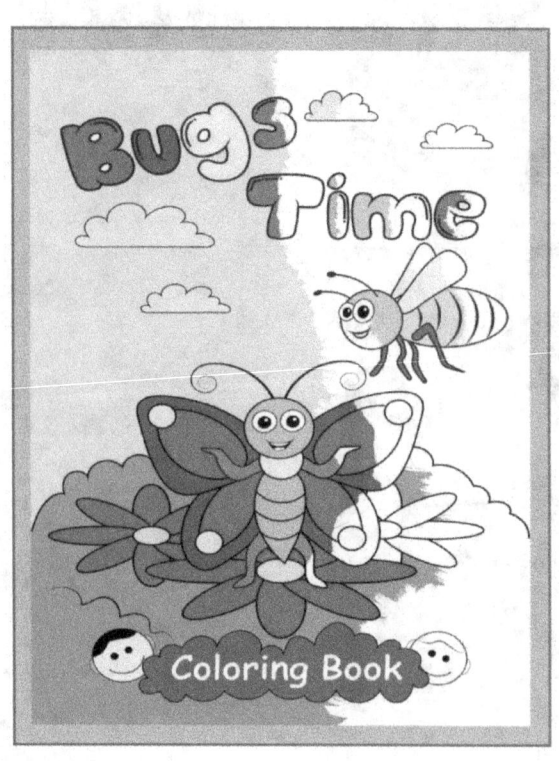

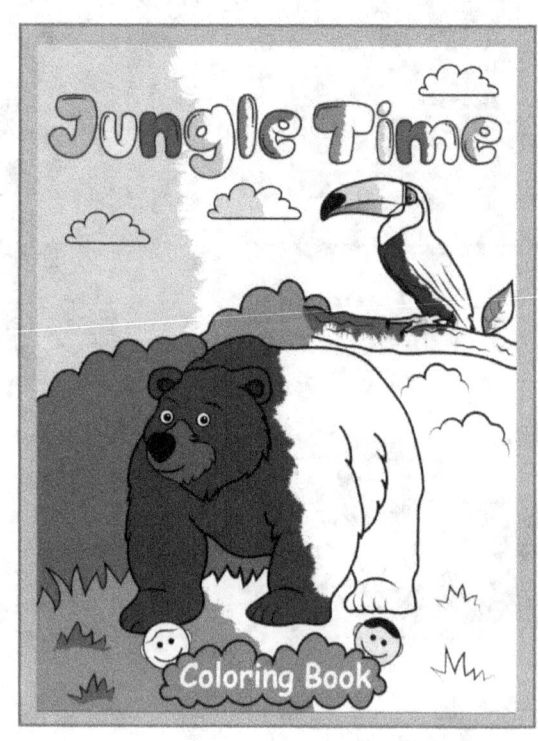

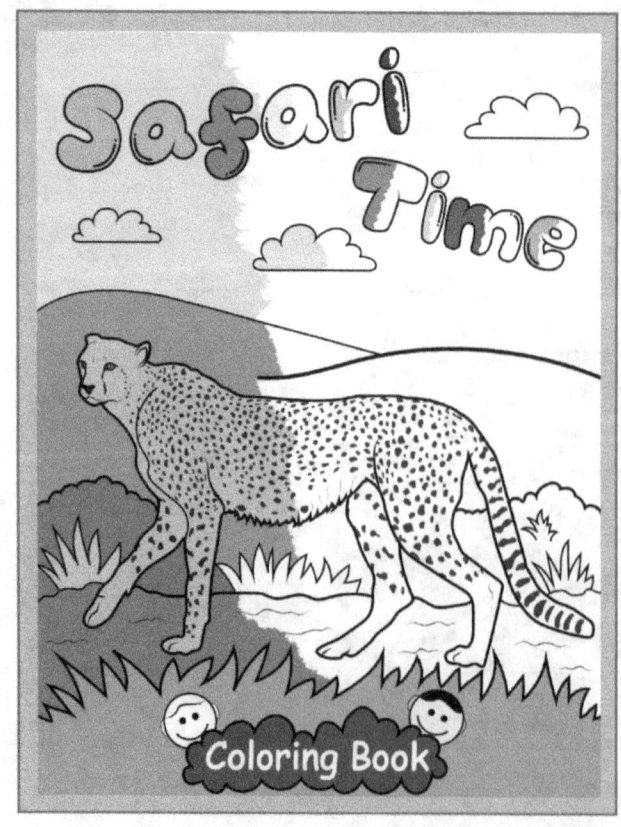

Visit **www.ArylaPublishing.com**
to find out about all new releases.

Follow us @arylapublishing on Twitter Instagram & Facebook

Search for Aryla Publishing on

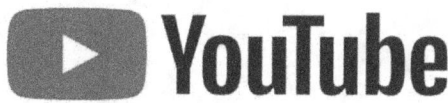 **YouTube**

Check out our <u>Book Trailers</u>

<u>Subscribe</u> to keep up to date with new releases!

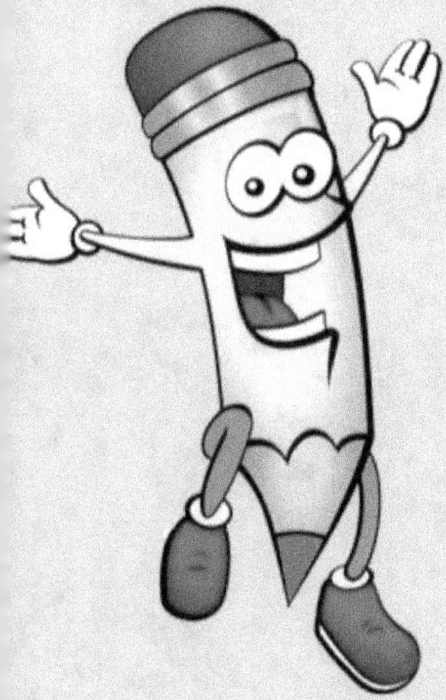

WE WOULD LOVE YOUR FEEDBACK

PLEASE LEAVE REVIEW AT:-

https://viewbook.at/mermaidreview